5 ingredient
Plant-Based Cookbook

76 EASY & DELICIOUS HIGH-PROTEIN RECIPES

J. Plants & Stephan Vogel

Version 1.1
eBook ASIN: B07Y6P9R3P
Paperback ISBN: 9789492788399
Hardcover ISBN: 9789492788405

INTRODUCTION

Congratulations!

With these 76 high-protein recipes, each one focusing on maximum flavor for minimal hassle, sorting out your daily food intake will become a virtually effortless task. Getting the right balance of calories and protein will become a lot easier with this collection of dishes at your fingertips, and if you try out the wide range of substitute ingredients and tips there are enough variations in this book to last a lifetime.

The dishes in this cookbook were created by J. Plants (@j.plantsss) from HappyHealthyGreen, and mainly use whole food ingredients. All the recipes are oil-free, rich in protein and require a maximum of five ingredients – mainly simple ones that can be easily stored. Working with a limited number of ingredients in the kitchen frees you from an overflowing pantry and late-night supermarket runs, and keeps the recipes straightforward.

Before you get going with these tasty meals, make sure you take the time to read the information chapters in the book first. You'll learn a great deal about the basics of nutrition and pick up useful data that will help you keep your pantry up to date. The chapter 'Tools & tips for quick and efficient cooking' will help you pick and use kitchen tools that will make your food preparation tasks stress-free.

An active lifestyle becomes more easily manageable with this approach, as the recipes in this cookbook require just a handful of ingredients and minimal effort. If you're serious about your results and want to take the next step, we offer standard and custom high-protein meal plans that incorporate these and other easy-to-prepare dishes. For more information and pricing, check out both our free and paid plans on our website here:

http://happyhealthygreen.life/meal-plans

TABLE OF CONTENTS

THE BASICS

Plant-based? Whole foods?

All ingredients in this book come from plants, along with a fungus or two here and there. The recipes rely mostly on whole foods that have undergone minimal processing. The use of salt is minimized, and dishes are free from oil and refined sugar.

What exactly is a diet high in protein?

A high-protein diet is one that is clearly abundant in amino acids. For a dish to qualify as '**high-protein**', we need to consider the amount of protein relative to the number of calories in the meal. As a rule of thumb, around 15 to 25% of the calories in a dish should come from protein in order for it to be labeled as '**high-protein**'.

Since one gram of protein is good for 4 calories, a minimum of 4 to 6 grams of protein per 100 calories is needed to make a meal that is high in protein. For a grown adult of average size, interested in growing muscle, this comes down to a rough average of 30 grams of protein per meal or serving. Depending on your size, your goals and the number of times you eat in a day, a single meal could pack as much as 60 grams of protein.

You'll find that carb-rich ingredients are often used in limited amounts (carb is short for carbohydrate, a macronutrient that provides 4 calories per gram). Recipes in this book are also free from oil, an ingredient that is very high in fat. Fat is already abundant in many natural ingredients, and provides a whopping 9 calories per single gram.

Oil-free cooking – how does that even work?

If you have never cooked without oil before, this might come as something of a surprise: cooking and baking without oil is perfectly possible, and you won't have to compromise on flavor. Getting rid of those extra calories from oils will also help you get in shape and stay lean.

Items such as a non-stick frying pan will make oil-free cooking a lot easier, and water will help you get started too as it prevents ingredients from burning. Make sure you stir frequently while cooking to stop ingredients sticking to the pan.

Now and then you might want to bring a little oil back in your life. And even though all recipes in this cookbook are designed to be cooked oil-free, they can also be prepared with oil. If you choose to do so, pick a cooking spray that is low in calories or try to keep the amount of oil used to an absolute minimum. Olive oil and coconut oil are your healthiest choices due to their high smoke points.

I have an allergy or food intolerance; can I still enjoy the recipes in this book?

You'll find a variety of recipes in this cookbook that are allergen-friendly or suggest substitute ingredients in the instructions. The chapter '**The plant-based high protein pantry & fridge**' offers a complete list of the ingredients used throughout this book, including various allergen-friendly substitutes.

Will cooking with only FIVE ingredients get boring over time?

Recipes in this book are all about *flavor without effort*. That's why not a single dish in this book requires more than five ingredients (optional toppings excluded). Some dishes rely on five whole food ingredients, whereas others call for lightly processed ingredients and a spice mix. By picking from all these options, you'll have a lifetime of tasty and nourishing meals available to you. The various substitute options and easy optional toppings also allow you to experiment with different flavors throughout the years of enjoying this cookbook.

And in case you do start to get bored at some point, remember this good news: the money you will save with these five-ingredient recipes will allow you to eat out virtually every weekend!

Are recipes in this book really that budget-friendly?

The short answer is yes! Working with only five ingredients really helps you to save on your grocery bill and, maybe more importantly, prevents waste as you'll have fewer unfinished items laying around. However, some ingredients might be more exclusive and expensive in your area and not practical or affordable to buy online. Keep an eye out for these ingredients and avoid recipes that rely on them if necessary!

Can recipes in this cookbook be halved, or doubled?

The meal serving sizes in this book are optimized for people that eat several meals per day. If you're trying to cut portion sizes, eat more frequently, or cater for two, you can simply halve or double the amount of servings. By halving or doubling the ingredients, you will be able to make half or twice the amount of total servings listed in the recipe. Decreasing or increasing the ingredients in a recipe typically does not require a change in cook time. However, if the thickness or density of certain dishes is affected, cook the recipe slightly for a shorter time when halved, or longer when doubled.

THE PLANT-BASED HIGH PROTEIN PANTRY & FRIDGE

Not all ingredients are equal, but that does not mean that the most expensive ingredient is automatically the better choice. Choosing a brand can make a difference worth mentioning, as processed products such as smoked tofu are subject to production processes that are unique to different companies. Freshness is another important aspect and the people working at your local farmers' market or supermarket will usually be able to tell you all the details.

The plant-based high-protein pantry

Protein sources		
Tofu (extra-firm) 13.5 gr. protein per 100 grams soy	The culinary possibilities of extra-firm and regular firm tofu are similar, but extra-firm tofu absorbs less flavor from marinades. Tofu is a versatile and affordable source of plant proteins with all nine essential amino acids plus fiber, calcium, and iron. *Used in '**Fried Rice with Tofu Scramble**' & '**Marinated Mushroom Scramble**'.*	**Substitutes:** *chickpea tofu and hempfu (soy-free)*
Tofu (smoked) 14.5 gr. protein per 100 grams soy	Extra-firm tofu with a smoky flavor that adds a delightful aroma to your dishes. *Used in '**Smoky Cajun Bowl**' & '**Split Pea Soup**'.*	**Substitutes:** *chickpea tofu and hempfu (soy-free) with a few drops of liquid smoke*
Tempeh 20 gr. protein per 100 grams soy	A traditional Indonesian fermented soybean product that is rich in protein and easy to digest. Tempeh is very versatile as it can be marinated and is a source of fiber, calcium, and iron. *Used in '**BBQ-LT Sandwich**', '**Mango Satay Tempeh Bowl**' & '**Tempeh Chili**'.*	**Substitutes:** *chickpea tempeh, black bean tempeh, and white bean tempeh (all of which are soy-free)*

T.V.P. *(Textured Vegetable Protein)* *48 gr. protein per 100 grams* soy	Textured vegetable protein is a defatted soy flour product that makes an excellent plant-based alternative to meat. It's budget-friendly and a source of all essential amino acids, fiber, calcium, and iron. *Used in recipes that require a meatless (soy) mince.*	**Substitutes:** *meatless (soy-free) mince, quinoa, bulgur, and millet*
Soy curls *33 gr. protein per 100 grams* soy	Soy curls are a meat alternative with a unique flavor and a texture similar to chicken. It's a versatile ingredient that makes a great protein and fiber source and includes calcium and iron. *Used in recipes that require soy curls.*	**Substitutes:** *meatless (soy-free) mince, T.V.P., quinoa, bulgur, and millet*
Meatless mince *22 gr. protein per 100 grams* soy	This mince is made with one or more plant-protein extracts, usually from soy or peas. It's sold as 'vegan meat' and is a tasty, easy-to-prepare source of protein. **Most products are soy-based but there are pea-based (soy-free) varieties available as well.** *Used in 'Mac 'n' Mince' & 'Sloppy Cajun Burgers'.*	**Substitutes:** *soy curls, T.V.P., quinoa, bulgur, and millet*
Seitan *75 gr. protein per 100 grams* gluten	Seitan is a tasty and nutritious product made from vital wheat gluten. It is versatile, cheap to make at home and includes micronutrients such as iron and calcium. *Seitan is a great soy-free substitute for tofu or other soy-based protein sources.*	**Substitutes:** *soy curls, T.V.P., tempeh, and tofu*

Beans & legumes

Chickpeas *21 gr. protein per 100 grams (dry)*	Chickpeas, also known as garbanzo beans, are a cheap and versatile ingredient that make an excellent source of protein, fiber, iron, vitamin B6, and magnesium. *Used in* **'Chorizo Chickpea Bowl'**, **'Tomato Curry Fritters'** & **'Chana Masala'**.	**Substitutes:** *white beans, pinto beans, and split peas*
Red lentils *22 gr. protein per 100 grams (dry)*	Red lentils are a tasty source of plant proteins and cook quickly as they're usually split. These inexpensive lentils are slightly sweet and a source of fiber, potassium, folate, and iron. *Used in* **'Red Lentil Dahl'**, **'Lentil Balls Pasta'** & **'Mango Lentil Salad'**.	**Substitutes:** *green lentils, kidney beans, and split peas*
Green lentils *20 gr. protein per 100 grams (dry)*	The most common type of lentil has a mild, earthy flavor and holds its shape well. They are very affordable and an excellent source of fiber, folate, and manganese. *Used in* **'Spicy Lentil Burgers'**, **'Lentil Mushroom Soup'** & **'Green Lentil Salad'**.	**Substitutes:** *chickpeas, split peas, and pinto beans*
Black beans *21 gr. protein per 100 grams (dry)*	Cheap, soft and creamy beans that absorb other flavors quite well. These legumes are a good protein and fiber source, and contain phosphorus, folate, and magnesium. *Used in* **'Sloppy Cajun Burgers'**, **'Black Bean Mushroom Burgers'** & **'Sweet Potato Tacos'**.	**Substitutes:** *kidney beans and pinto beans*
Split peas *25 gr. protein per 100 grams (dry)*	The peeled and split seeds of peas have a short cooking time and turn very creamy when cooked through. Green split peas are less starchy and sweeter than the milder yellow split peas. Both are affordable, versatile ingredients that contain fiber, potassium, vitamin B1, and magnesium. *Used in* **'Split Pea Tempeh Burgers'** & **'Split Pea Soup'**.	**Substitutes:** *chickpeas, pinto beans, and green lentils*
White beans *24 gr. protein per 100 grams (dry)*	'White beans' is a collective name for navy beans, Great Northern beans, cannellini beans and baby lima beans. In Europe, this name commonly refers to navy beans or cannellini beans. White beans are cheap and an excellent source of fiber, vitamin B1, zinc, copper, and manganese. *Used in* **'White Beans Summer Salad'** & **'Provencal Beans & Tomato Salad'**.	**Substitutes:** *pinto beans, chickpeas, and soybeans*
Pinto beans *20 gr. protein per 100 grams (dry)*	Popular and versatile beans with a lightly crunchy consistency and nutty, earthy flavor. Pinto beans take on the flavors of the ingredients they are paired with, and are a cheap source of fiber, iron, zinc, calcium, and selenium. *Used for chilis, soups, and in* **'Pinto Salsa Bowl'**.	**Substitutes:** *chickpeas, black beans, and pinto beans*

Beans & legumes

Navy beans 20 gr. protein per 100 grams (dry)	Navy beans are small white beans with a mild, delicate nut-like flavor. They are inexpensive, and an excellent source of dietary fiber, vitamin B1, zinc, copper, and manganese. Used in '**White Beans Summer Salad**' & '**Provencal Beans & Tomato Salad**'.	**Substitutes:** *pinto beans, chickpeas, and soybeans*

Carb sources

Basmati rice 5 gr. protein per 100 grams (uncooked)	A variety of long-grain, soft rice with a light nutty flavor and floral aroma. Basmati rice is easy to digest and also a source of B-vitamins, iron, folate, and manganese. Great with '**Chana Masala**' & '**Red Lentil Dahl**'.	**Substitutes:** *quinoa, amaranth, millet, and buckwheat*
(Quick-cooking) brown rice 7 gr. protein per 100 grams (uncooked)	Brown rice is used in multiple flavorful dishes and has a firm, chewy texture with an almost nutty flavor. It's very affordable and is a good source of fiber, manganese, and magnesium. Great with '**Smoky Cajun Bowl**' & '**Lentil Rice Soup**'.	**Substitutes:** *quinoa, amaranth, millet, and buckwheat*
Brown rice noodles 10 gr. protein per 100 grams	Noodles made from brown rice that taste a little nuttier than white rice noodles. Brown rice noodles are less starchy and a little less chewy than wheat noodles and are a good source of fiber, manganese, and magnesium. A great staple for quick and easy dishes and used in '**Soy Mince Noodle Bowl**'.	**Substitutes:** *shirataki noodles and whole wheat noodles*
Buckwheat flour 9 gr. protein per 100 grams	This gluten-free flour has a nutty, slightly earthy flavor that gives your baking more taste and complexity. It is an affordable ingredient and a source of fiber, vitamin B1, magnesium, and zinc. A gluten-free substitute for oats and used in '**Buckwheat Protein Bread**'.	**Substitutes:** *chickpea flour, lentil flour, whole wheat flour, and oat flour*
Couscous 12 gr. protein per 100 grams (uncooked) gluten	These granules of durum wheat are available in various sizes and have a fluffy, light consistency that gets its flavor from spices and other ingredients. Couscous is relatively cheap and a source of fiber, vitamin B1, vitamin B3, and manganese. Great in salads and used in '**Fiery Couscous salad**'.	**Substitutes:** *quinoa, bulgur, buckwheat, amaranth, and brown rice*

Carb sources

Instant oats *14 gr. protein per 100 grams (uncooked)*	These fast-cooking oats are a versatile and cheap ingredient that is packed with fiber, magnesium, vitamin B1, and zinc. Look for unflavored oats without added sugar, colorings, or other ingredients. *Used in '**Apple Cinnamon Oats Bowl**' & '**Oats 'n' Raisins cookies**'.*	**Substitutes:** *buckwheat, millet, and grits*
Quinoa *14 gr. protein per 100 grams (uncooked)*	Quinoa is a gluten-free, nutrient-packed grain that is fluffy, creamy, crunchy and somewhat nutty when cooked. It can be eaten warm or cold and contains the minerals magnesium, manganese, and phosphorus. *Used in '**Pineapple Quinoa Salad**', '**Chickpea Apple Salad**' & '**Quinoa Almond Cookies**'.*	**Substitutes:** *brown rice, green lentils, amaranth, and bulgur*
Sweet potatoes *2 gr. protein per 100 grams*	Starchy, flavorful, sweet-tasting root vegetables that are lower in calories than regular potatoes. These potatoes are a natural sweetener and a source of fiber, vitamin A, vitamin C, and potassium. *Used in '**Sweet Potato Tacos**', '**Sweet Potato & Broccoli Bowl**' & '**Creamy Asparagus & Sweet Potatoes**'.*	**Substitutes:** *regular potatoes*
Whole wheat flour *14 gr. protein per 100 grams (uncooked)* gluten	This powder is made by grinding whole grains of wheat and is widely used in bakery products. It has a tasty, nutty flavor and is a good source of fiber, vitamin B1, vitamin B3, and manganese. *Used in '**Vanilla Protein Pancakes**' & '**High Protein Muffins**'.*	**Substitutes:** *chickpea flour, lentil flour, buckwheat flour, and oat flour*
Whole wheat pasta *14 gr. protein per 100 grams (uncooked)* gluten	Pasta made from whole wheat flour is a staple ingredient with a nutty flavor that goes well with the acidity of tomatoes. The fiber-rich pasta contains minerals such as vitamin B1, vitamin B3, and manganese. *Used in '**Mac 'n' Mince**', '**Spaghetti Bolognese**' & '**Red Lentil Pasta**'.*	**Substitutes:** *lentil pasta, black bean pasta, and chickpea pasta*

Nuts & seeds

Flaxseeds *18 gr. protein per 100 grams*	Available in brown, with an earthy, nutty taste, or golden, with a smooth and nutty taste. These cheap, nutritious seeds can be used as an ingredient or topping and are an excellent source of fiber, omega 3, antioxidants, lignans, and folate. *Used in '**Choco Berry Pudding**' & '**Chocolate Avocado Smoothie**'.*	**Substitutes:** *hemp seeds, chia seeds, and walnuts*
Chia seeds *17 gr. protein per 100 grams*	Chia seeds have a mild, nutty flavor and can absorb 12 times their weight in water, which changes their consistency from crunchy and dense to a texture like that of tapioca pearls. The seeds are a good source of fiber, omega 3, antioxidants, iron, and calcium. *Used in '**Gingerbread Smoothie**' & '**Buckwheat Protein Bread**'.*	**Substitutes:** *flax seeds, hemp seeds, and walnuts*
Almonds *25 gr. protein per 100 grams* nuts	Almonds have a crunchy texture and a neutral taste that's slightly buttery and sweet. They are a versatile ingredient and a source of fiber, vitamin E, manganese, and magnesium. *Used in '**Coconut Crumble Bars**', '**Choco Almond Bars**' & '**Paleo Power Bread**'.*	**Substitutes:** *peanuts and pumpkin seeds*
Peanuts *26 gr. protein per 100 grams*	Raw peanuts have a bland taste, but when roasted, these legumes have a sweet flavor with nutty notes. Choose all-natural (roasted) peanuts, which are affordable and contain omega 6, potassium, magnesium, and vitamin E. *Great in salads, or as a quick (high-calorie) protein snack. Used as a topping in '**Black Pepper Tempeh Stir-fry**'.*	**Substitutes:** *almonds, cashews, and sunflower seeds*
Pistachios *20 gr. protein per 100 grams* nuts	These mild, sweet nuts contain fiber, potassium, antioxidants, vitamin B6, and melatonin. *Used in '**Pistachio Protein Ice Cream**' & '**Red Lentil Pasta**'.*	**Substitutes:** *almonds, cashews, and pumpkin seeds*
Cashews *20 gr. protein per 100 grams* nuts	Sweet and buttery nuts that taste best roasted and are packed with iron, magnesium, and vitamin B6. Chooses raw or roasted cashews with only salt added. *Used in '**Cashew Cream Cheese**' & '**Lemon Pie Bars**'.*	**Substitutes:** *almonds, peanuts, and sunflower seeds*

Nuts & seeds

Hazelnuts *15 gr. protein per 100 grams* nuts	Hazelnuts are salty/sweet with notes of butter and have a crisp, rich texture. These nuts are a good source of fiber, vitamin E, manganese, copper, and vitamin B6. *Used in '**Hazelnut Choco Plum Bites**'.*	**Substitutes:** *peanuts, cashews, and almonds*
Pumpkin seeds *32 gr. protein per 100 grams*	The dried seeds of a pumpkin have a sweet, nutty flavor, and a crunchy texture when roasted. They are affordable and packed with vitamin K, manganese, iron, and zinc. *Used in '**Paleo Power Bread**'.*	**Substitutes:** *sunflower seeds, almonds, and peanuts*
Sunflower seeds *21 gr. protein per 100 grams*	Sunflower seeds have a mild, nutty flavor and taste better roasted than raw. They are inexpensive and contain omega 6, iron, vitamin B6, and magnesium. *Used in '**Paleo Power Bread**'.*	**Substitutes:** *pumpkin seeds, almonds, and peanuts*
Sesame seeds *18 gr. protein per 100 grams*	These crunchy seeds have a subtle nutty taste, are affordable and make a nutritious topping. Sesame seeds are a good source of fiber, calcium, iron, and vitamin B6.	**Substitutes:** *sunflower seeds, almonds, and peanuts*
Peanut butter *26 gr. protein per 100 grams* peanuts	Butter made from peanuts with a sweet, nutty flavor. Choose a 100% natural peanut butter without any additives other than salt. *Used in '**Mango Satay Tempeh Bowl**' & '**Peanut Butter Chocolate Bars**'.*	**Substitutes:** *tahini, almond butter, and cashew butter*
Tahini *21 gr. protein per 100 grams*	A paste made from sesame seeds that has a delightful flavor similar to peanut butter but available 100% nut-free. It is full of healthy fats, vitamins, and minerals. *Used in '**Chickpea Apple Salad**' & '**Lemon Garlic Chickpea Salad**'.*	**Substitutes:** *peanut butter, almond butter, and sunflower seed butter*
Almond butter *25 gr. protein per 100 grams* nuts	A creamy, silky nut butter made from almonds. Almond butter is a source of potassium, calcium, manganese, and magnesium. *Great as a topping and used in '**Choco Almond Mousse Pudding**'.*	**Substitutes:** *peanut butter, cashew butter, and sunflower seed butter*

Vegetables & fresh produce

A well-stocked pantry includes vegetables and fresh produce. Most veggies are inexpensive and low in calories; they are also rich in fiber and pack loads of vitamins and minerals. Depending on the vegetable, they also contain a certain amount of protein and add color and flavor to dishes. Most can be eaten raw, although some must undergo some processing before they are used in a recipe.

Keep fresh veggies and produce you're planning to use the same day in the fridge, and freeze vegetables you're planning to use at a later date. Alternatively, buy frozen veggies that maintain their nutritional value better over longer periods of time, are cheaper in bulk and can be kept in the freezer for long periods of time.

✓ Asparagus	✓ Carrots	✓ Endive	✓ Kale	✓ Sauerkraut
✓ Bell peppers	✓ Celery	✓ Garlic	✓ Lettuce	✓ Sweet corn
✓ Broccoli	✓ Cherry tomatoes	✓ Ginger	✓ Olives	✓ Tomatoes
✓ Button Mushrooms	✓ Cucumber	✓ Green peas	✓ Onions	

Fruits

Fruits include the most nutritious sweets that nature has to offer. All the listed fruits can be eaten raw as a simple snack, but also make a wonderful ingredient in recipes. Just like vegetables, they are rich in fiber, vitamins, and minerals. Fruits contain a relatively low amount of protein, but sweet fruits such as bananas, dates, mango, and raisins are excellent ingredients for masking bitter flavors, such as the taste of unflavored pea protein powder.Fresh fruits without a thick peel are best kept in the fridge and consumed or used in a recipe as soon as possible after purchase. Frozen fruits are an affordable staple, especially if you buy in bulk, and preserve their nutrition better over time, making them the better choice unless you have access to freshly picked fruits every day of the week.

✓ Apples	✓ Cherries	✓ Kiwis	✓ Pineapples	✓ Raisins
✓ Avocados	✓ Coconut	✓ Lemons	✓ Plums	✓ Strawberries
✓ Bananas	✓ Cranberries	✓ Mango	✓ Raspberries	✓ Tangerines
✓ Blueberries	✓ Dates	✓ Oranges		

Herbs & spices

Herbs and spices are indispensable ingredients in the kitchen as they add flavor to your dishes like no other cooking component can. A collection of quality dried spices will always come in handy, and usually keep their potency for up to 6 months or longer. Depending on the dish, some herbs and spices are better when they are bought fresh. Fresh herbs are sold freshly cut or in a pot complete with their roots. Note that fresh herbs have a limited shelf life and are best kept in the fridge if you're planning to use them the same day. Otherwise, it's best to (partially) dehydrate and freeze freshly cut herbs. For the freshest possible herbs, harvest them directly from the plant directly before or during cooking. Herb plants are commonly sold in supermarkets.

As a rule of thumb, store all dried herbs and spices in a cool, dark place and use cut herbs as soon as possible after purchasing or harvesting.

- ✓ 5-spice powder
- ✓ Basil
- ✓ Black pepper
- ✓ Burger spices
- ✓ Cajun spices (salt-free)
- ✓ Chili flakes
- ✓ Cilantro
- ✓ Cinnamon
- ✓ Cumin seeds
- ✓ Curry spices
- ✓ Garlic powder
- ✓ Green peppercorns
- ✓ Italian herbs
- ✓ Mexican chili spice mix
- ✓ Mexican chorizo seasoning
- ✓ Mint
- ✓ Onion powder
- ✓ Oregano
- ✓ Paprika powder
- ✓ Parsley
- ✓ Provencal herbs
- ✓ Ras El Hanout
- ✓ Rosemary
- ✓ Kosher or sea salt
- ✓ Smoked paprika
- ✓ Thyme
- ✓ Turmeric
- ✓ Vanilla extract

Condiments and others

Condiments and the other ingredients listed here are used to add flavor, nutrition and substance to dishes in this book. All these ingredients have long shelf lives, and lemons and limes can be kept fresh in the fridge for up to a month. Your pantry should always include vegetable stock, which can bring flavor to even the plainest foods.

- ✓ Almond flakes
- ✓ Almond flakes (unsweetened)
- ✓ Apple cider vinegar
- ✓ Balsamic vinegar
- ✓ Coconut cream
- ✓ Coconut milk
- ✓ Cocoa powder
- ✓ Dark chocolate (dairy-free)
- ✓ Dill pickle slices
- ✓ Lemon garlic pepper seasoning
- ✓ Lemon juice
- ✓ Lime juice
- ✓ Low-sodium soy sauce
- ✓ Nutritional yeast
- ✓ Pickled vegetables
- ✓ Soy sauce
- ✓ Sweet soy sauce
- ✓ Teriyaki sauce
- ✓ Vegetable stock

TOOLS & TIPS FOR QUICK AND EFFICIENT COOKING

Food processor

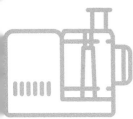

This is one of the most versatile tools you can possibly have in your kitchen – it can shred, chop, slice, grind, puree, and blend, all with the simple press of a button. With this machine you'll be able to make dough for your burger patties, batter for your protein bars, and a whole range of nut butters, hummus, and guacamole. In this book, you'll find several recipes that can be prepared easily with the help of a food processor.

Note: *When making dough from beans and/or legumes, it is always recommended that you soak and cook dry beans, rather than using pre-cooked ingredients from a jar or can.*

Food processor recipes:

Breakfasts: *Paleo Power Bread, Buckwheat Protein Bread.*
Meals: *Tempeh Split Pea Burgers, Moroccan Chickpea Rolls, Black Bean Quinoa Burgers, Tomato Curry Fritters, Spicy Lentil Burgers, Black Bean Mushroom Burgers, Mexican Chorizo Loaf.*
Snacks: *Hazelnut Choco Plum Bites, Coconut Crumble Bars, Choco Almond Bars, Oats 'n' Raisins Cookies, Lemon Pie Bars, Almond Cookie Balls, Gingerbread Protein Bars, Peanut Butter Chocolate Bars, Quinoa Almond Cookies.*

Blender

Liquid or easy-to-chew meals like smoothies or smoothie bowls are cornerstones of a plant-based diet that's high in protein and also time-efficient. The blender allows you simply to dump healthy ingredients, including protein powder, into the container with enough water and/or plant milk – and with the press of a button, you'll get a colorful, tasty smoothie in return. This tool is also heaven-sent when it comes to creating delicious soups, sauces and dips.

Blender recipes:

Breakfasts: *Vanilla Protein Pancakes, Choco Berry Pudding, Chocolate Avocado Smoothie, Mango Choco Protein Pudding, Choco Almond Mousse Pudding, Gingerbread Smoothie, Orange Sunrise Smoothie, Strawberry Banana Smoothie.*
Salads: *Mango Lentil Salad.*
Soups: *Provencal Lentil Soup.*
Snacks: *High-protein Muffins, Pistachio Protein Ice Cream.*

Immersion (hand) blender

The immersion blender allows you to blend smoothies, soups, stews and sauces in the pot without having to transfer the food to a separate container. It is basically a stick with blender blades that can do almost everything the regular blender can, while also cutting down on the amount of washing-up you have to do. As an extra bonus it's only small, so you can take it anywhere for food on the move!

Hand blender recipes:

All of the regular blender recipes.

Breakfasts: *Paleo Power Bread, Buckwheat Protein Bread.*
Snacks: *Hazelnut Choco Plum Bites, Coconut Crumble Bars, Choco Almond Bars, Oats 'n' Raisins Cookies, Lemon Pie Bars, Almond Cookie Balls, Gingerbread Protein Bars, Peanut Butter Chocolate Bars, Quinoa Almond Cookies.*

Potato masher

If you don't have access to a food processor or blender, a potato masher makes a good cheap alternative. By channeling some human effort instead of electricity, you can easily mash ingredients into hummus, guacamole, salsa and dough for bean burger patties. A potato masher could be a lifesaver when you're enjoying a weekend camping trip and want to mash some beans, tahini and spices into a quick plant-based high-protein meal.

Potato masher recipes:

Meals: *Tempeh Split Pea Burgers, Moroccan Chickpea Rolls, Black Bean Quinoa Burgers, Tomato Curry Fritters, Spicy Lentil Burgers, Black Bean Mushroom Burgers, Mexican Chorizo Loaf.*

Handheld mixer

As an alternative, the classic handheld mixer can be very useful and will save you a lot of time. Preparing recipes such as *Buckwheat Protein Bread, Vanilla Protein Pancakes, Protein Muffins, Oats 'n' Raisins Cookies* and *Pistachio Protein Ice Cream* is a piece of cake with this handy kitchen device. The mixer also lends itself to whipping up some coconut cream or creating a quick tahini dressing without the risk of injuring your wrist.

Handheld mixer recipes:

Breakfasts: *Buckwheat Protein Bread, Vanilla Protein Pancakes, Choco Berry Pudding, Chocolate Avocado Smoothie, Mango Choco Protein Pudding, Choco Almond Mousse Pudding, Gingerbread Smoothie, Orange Sunrise Smoothie, Strawberry Banana Smoothie.*
Snacks: *Protein Muffins, Oats 'n' Raisins cookies, Pistachio Protein Ice Cream.*

Non-stick frying pan

Last but certainly not least is the non-stick frying pan. This is a must-have for oil-free cooking as it allows you to sauté and stir-fry without the need to add any oil. With only a splash of water, onions and garlic get that wonderful sautéed aroma without any extra calories. This pan alone will help you cut hundreds of calories per day compared to the traditional sautéing method that relies on oil.

To cook completely oil-free with this pan, heat it up and add 2 tablespoons of water or vegetable stock, followed by the ingredients that you would like to sauté. Make sure to stir often and, if necessary, add an additional tablespoon of water during cooking to prevent sticking and burning.

Note that soy-based products such as tofu, TVP, soy mince and tempeh will soak up water when being cooked without oil. Compared to veggies that contain a lot of water, these ingredients will most likely need some additional liquid to prevent them from sticking to the pan. It's a good idea to use just a medium heat when frying these soy products without oil.

Non-stick frying pan recipes:

Meals: *Fried Rice with Tofu Scramble, Soy Mince Noodle Bowl, Marinated Mushroom Scramble, Mac 'n' Mince, Smoky Cajun Bowl, Sweet Potato Tacos, Provencal Broccoli Bowl, Sweet Potato & Broccoli Bowl, Red Lentil Pasta, Lentil Balls Pasta, Black Pepper Tempeh Stir-fry, Chorizo Chickpea Bowl.*

Quality, brands and pricing

Not all tools and utensils offer the same level of usability – different brands and models will all come with a slightly different range of properties.

To help you choose the one that's right for you, we've reviewed a number of must-have tools. Check out these product reviews on our website here:

http://happyhealthygreen.life/product-reviews

Where we have included everything from budget smoothie blenders to quality all-round blenders and other equipment.

SOAKING AND COOKING STAPLE FOODS

A well-stocked pantry also includes several dry, plant-based whole foods with a long shelf life. The perfect pantry should include ingredients used in this book, such as beans, lentils and grains like rice and quinoa. These ingredients add texture, flavor and fiber to dishes and are packed with protein and other nutrients; they're also extremely affordable when you buy in bulk.

All these staples – particularly beans and lentils – contain phytic acid, a natural substance found in plant seeds that protects them from insect attack and stops them sprouting too early. Unless you're buying your beans and lentils pre-cooked, it's essential to reduce the level of phytic acid in these legumes, as consuming too much of it will impair the absorption of important micronutrients like calcium, magnesium, copper, zinc, and iron. The consumption of large doses of phytic acid can even result in serious malnutrition and disrupted gut health, so it really is very important to decrease their presence in legumes.

Getting rid of most of the phytic acids in beans and lentils is quite easy, but it requires a bit of preparation. By soaking, rinsing and then cooking your ingredients properly, most of these acids will be flushed out. Doing this will improve the nutritional value of these staples, and all you need to do is leave them to soak for a relatively short period of time.

Soaking can be done overnight, or more quickly with some hot water. For the first method, fill a pot with plenty of water and add the beans or lentils. Make sure there is enough water in the pot, as these legumes can soak up three times their dry volume in water. After leaving the beans or lentils overnight, or for roughly 8 hours, discard the water, rinse the legumes, and cook them. Detailed soaking and cooking times for each legume type are shown in the chart below.

An alternative and faster method is basically very similar to the overnight method, but uses hot water. Simply heat the water in the pot until it comes to a boil, then turn down the heat to a point where the water is simmering softly and add your beans or lentils. For a quick soak, remove the pot from the heat after roughly an hour, get rid of the water, then rinse the legumes and prepare to cook them. For a proper hot soak, remove the pot after an hour, cover it with a lid and leave the legumes to sit for up to another 3 hours before draining the water and rinsing the legumes. Quick and hot soaks are not recommended for split ingredients, such as split peas and split red lentils.

Make sure to wash off any remaining indigestible sugars and phytic acids by giving the beans or lentils a good rinse before cooking them. Cooking is also best done with more than enough water, keeping the level at least 1 inch (2.5 cm) above the legumes. Partially cover the pot with a lid and aim for a gentle simmer to prevent the beans and legumes from breaking down. Cannellini, white kidney, and red beans need to be boiled for at least a few minutes to get rid of the natural poisons they contain.

Soaking and cooking time per legume

Legume (per 100 grams, dry)	Soaking time	Cooking time	Rough yield (cooked)
Black beans	8-12 hrs.	60-90 mins.	300 grams
Chickpeas	8-12 hrs.	1-3 hrs.	300 grams
White beans	8-12 hrs.	1½ hrs.	300 grams
Green split peas	0-4 hrs.	45 mins.	200 grams
Yellow split peas	0-4 hrs.	60-90 mins.	200 grams
Lentils, green	8-12 hrs.	30-45 mins.	300 grams
Lentils, red or yellow	8-12 hrs.	20-30 mins.	300 grams
Navy beans	6-8 hrs.	45-60 mins.	300 grams
Pinto beans	8-12 hrs.	1½ hrs.	300 grams
Soybeans	8-12 hrs.	1-2 hrs.	300 grams

*The recommended times in this chart are approximate.

You can tell that beans and lentils are properly cooked when they can be mashed without a lot of effort. Make sure to drain all the water after the beans or lentils are done cooking before you consume them, incorporate them in a recipe, or store them. Cool down the cooked legumes completely before storage, and keep them in the fridge in an airtight container.

Note: A pressure cooker can cook beans and legumes on demand and very quickly. An Instant Pot, for example, will cook beans or lentils about six times faster. Use one of these and what would normally take an hour now only takes 10 minutes. If you're interested in cooking with an electric pressure cooker, check out our website for more information and to see our Instant Pot cookbook!

Soaking small seeds

Chia seeds and flaxseeds are common ingredients that are best soaked prior to being consumed or used in a recipe. Soaking will not only transform their texture but also make it easier to digest these seeds and take advantage of their nutrients.

Soak chia seeds in a jar or bowl with roughly 12 times their weight in water, and stir occasionally to prevent the seeds from forming lumps. To fully soak the chia seeds, they will need at least an hour in the water, but an overnight soak combined with an occasional stir is ideal. Soaked chia seeds can be easily kept in the fridge for a couple of days.

Flaxseeds do not absorb water like chia seeds do but are also best soaked before consumption – used this way, they also make a perfect egg replacement. Soak flaxseeds in a jar or bowl with about twice their weight in water added. They should be soaked for at least 2 hours, or until the water turns opaque from the soluble fiber released by the flaxseeds.

1. PEANUT BUTTER APPLE SAUCE

Serves: 16   🕐 **Cook:** 15 min.   🕐 **Total:** 25 min.

INGREDIENTS:

4 large apples
(skinned, cored)

130 g. | ½ cup
Peanut butter

40 g. | ¼ cup
Raisins

10 g. | 1 tbsp.
Cinnamon

120 ml. | ½ cup
Water

ALLERGENS

Peanuts
(can be substituted
with almond butter)

METHOD:

1. Cut the cored and skinned apples into tiny pieces and add them to the saucepan.

2. Add the water to the saucepan and put it over low heat then cover the saucepan with a lid and bring it to a boil.

3. Cook the apples for about 15 minutes or until they are soft then turn off the heat and mash the apples with a fork or a potato masher.

4. Add the peanut butter and stir thoroughly until everything is well combined.

5. Add more water if the sauce is too thick, then add the raisins and cinnamon.

6. Stir again until everything is mixed thoroughly, serve warm or cold and enjoy!

7. Store the sauce in the fridge, using an airtight container, and consume within 3 days. Store the sauce in the freezer for a maximum of 60 days and thaw at room temperature.

TIP:

Add 1 cup of water to the food processor to create a sauce, and add smoked chipotles, cumin seeds and paprika powder for a quick and delicious nacho dip.

NOTE:

If you need to use pine nuts as a substitute, skip the first 3 steps and roast the pine nuts for 15 minutes at 257°F/125°C.

2. CASHEW CREAM CHEESE

INGREDIENTS:

200 g. | 2 cups
Raw cashews
(unsalted)

7 ml. | ½ tbsp.
Balsamic vinegar

40 g. | ¼ cup
Nutritional yeast

Salt and pepper to taste
(optional)

ALLERGENS

Cashews
(can be substituted
with pine nuts)

METHOD:

1. Half fill a saucepan with water, put it over medium high heat and bring it to a boil.

2. Add the cashews to the saucepan and boil them for 15 minutes.

3. Strain the cashews after boiling them, then discard the water and let them cool down completely.

4. Add all of the ingredients to a food processor and blend until smooth.

5. Serve the cashew cream cheese chilled and enjoy as a topping or a side!

6. Store the cream cheese in the fridge, using an airtight container, and consume within 4 days. Alternatively, store the cream cheese in the freezer for a maximum of 60 days and thaw at room temperature.

3. SOUR CREAM

INGREDIENTS:

300 g. | 1 cup
Coconut cream

30 ml. | 2 tbsp.
Lemon juice

7 ml. | ½ tsp.
Apple cider vinegar

2 g. | ½ tsp.
Salt
(optional)

METHOD:

1. Add all of the ingredients to a food processor or blender and blend until smooth.

   Alternatively, put all ingredients into a medium bowl and whisk using hand mixers until smooth.

2. Serve the sour cream chilled and enjoy as a topping or a side!

3. Store the sour cream in the fridge, using an airtight container, and consume within 4 days. Alternatively, store the sour cream in the freezer for a maximum of 60 days and thaw at room temperature.

4. SPICY TAHINI DRESSING

INGREDIENTS:

120 g. | ½ cup
Tahini

30 ml. | 2 tbsp.
Lemon juice

1 clove
Garlic
(minced)

10 g. | 1 tbsp.
Paprika powder

120 ml. | ½ cup
Water

METHOD:

1. Add all of the ingredients to a small bowl or a jar and whisk or shake until smooth.

2. Serve the tahini dressing chilled and enjoy as a topping or a side!

3. Store the tahini dressing in the fridge, using an airtight container, and consume within 4 days. Alternatively, store the tahini dressing in the freezer for a maximum of 60 days and thaw at room temperature.

TIP:
Add 2 tablespoons of lemon juice for a tangier flavor, and add smoked chipotles to give the sauce some extra kick.

5. BBQ SAUCE

INGREDIENTS:

360 g. | 2 cups
Tomato cubes
(canned or fresh)

5 dates
(pitted)

30 g. | 3 tbsp.
Smoked paprika

20 g. | 2 tbsp.
Garlic powder

20 g. | 2 tbsp.
Onion powder

METHOD:

1. Add all the ingredients to a blender or food processor and blend to form a smooth sauce.

2. Store the BBQ sauce in the fridge, using an airtight container, and consume within 3 days. Alternatively, store it in the freezer for a maximum of 60 days and thaw at room temperature.

6. MEXICAN SALSA

INGREDIENTS:

3 large tomatoes
(quartered)

¼ red onion
(chopped)

10 g. | ¼ cup
Fresh cilantro

1 jalapeno
1 clove

Garlic
(minced)

METHOD:

1. Remove the stem, seeds and placenta of the jalapeno and cut the flesh into slices.

2. Add all of the ingredients to a food processor or blender and blend until smooth.

3. Serve the salsa chilled and enjoy as a topping or a side!

4. Store the salsa in the fridge, using an airtight container, and consume within 3 days. Alternatively, store it in the freezer for a maximum of 60 days and thaw at room temperature.

7. SPICY SATAY SAUCE

Serves: 8   🕐 **Cook:** 10 min.   🕐 **Total:** 15 min.

INGREDIENTS:

260 g. | 1 cup
Peanut butter

30 ml. | 2 tbsp.
Lime juice

60 ml. | ¼ cup
Sweet soy sauce

2 small onions
(minced)

2 cloves
Garlic
(minced)

480 ml. | 2 cups
Water

OPTIONAL TOPPINGS:

Red chili flakes

Minced ginger

Fresh cilantro

ALLERGENS

Peanuts
(can be substituted
with almond butter)
Soy sauce (gluten)
(can be substituted with gluten-free
tamari or coconut aminos)

METHOD:

1. Put all ingredients in a food processor and blend until smooth, add more water if the sauce is too thick.

   Alternatively, mix everything in a medium bowl, using a handheld mixer.

2. Heat up the sauce in a saucepan over a medium heat. Let it cook for about 10 minutes while stirring continuously as the sauce thickens.

3. Turn off the heat and let the sauce cool down for a minute while stirring.

4. Serve warm with the optional toppings and enjoy!

5. Store the satay sauce in an airtight container in the fridge and consume within 4 days. The satay sauce can also be stored in the freezer for a maximum of 90 days. Thaw at room temperature before serving.

8. COCONUT WHIPPED CREAM

INGREDIENTS:

300 g. | 1 cup
Coconut cream

10 ml. | 1 tsp.
Vanilla extract

20 g. | 2 tbsp.
Cocoa powder
(optional)

METHOD:

1. Add all of the ingredients to large bowl and mix for about 5 minutes using an electrical mixer with beaters or a whisk.

2. Serve the whipped cream chilled and enjoy as a topping or a side!

3. Store the whipped cream in the fridge, using an airtight container, and consume within 2 days. Alternatively, store the whipped cream in the freezer for a maximum of 60 days and thaw at room temperature.

9. LEMON MINT TAHINI CREAM

INGREDIENTS:

120 g. | ½ cup
Tahini

3 dates
(pitted)

120 ml. | ½ cup
Water

60 ml. | ¼ cup
Lemon juice

2 cloves
Garlic

6 leaves
Mint

METHOD:

1. Add all the ingredients to a blender or food processor and blend to form a thick and smooth sauce.

2. Store the tahini cream in the fridge, using an airtight container, and consume within 3 days. Alternatively, store the tahini cream in the freezer for a maximum of 60 days and thaw at room temperature.

10. EASY GUACAMOLE

INGREDIENTS:

2 large Hass avocadoes
(peeled, stoned, halved)

60 ml. | ¼ cup
Lemon juice

1 red onion
(minced)

1 clove
Garlic
(minced)

15 g. | ½ cup
Fresh cilantro
(chopped)

OPTIONAL TOPPINGS:

Jalapeno slices

Sweet corn

METHOD:

1. Put all ingredients in a food processor and blend until smooth.

   Alternatively, for a chunky guacamole, mash the ingredients in a medium-sized bowl with a fork.

2. Serve right away with the optional toppings and enjoy!

3. Store the guacamole in an airtight container in the fridge and consume within 2 days. Alternatively, store in the freezer for a maximum of 90 days, and thaw at room temperature before serving.

11. POMEGRANATE GINGER SAUCE

INGREDIENTS:

320 g. | 2 cups
Pomegranate seeds
(fresh or frozen)

10 dried plums
(pitted)

20 g. | 2-inch piece
Ginger

10 g. | 1 tbsp.
Black pepper

METHOD:

1. Add all the ingredients to a blender or food processor and blend to form a smooth sauce.

2. Store the pomegranate sauce in the fridge, using an airtight container and consume within 3 days. Alternatively, store it in the freezer for a maximum of 60 days and thaw at room temperature.

BREAKFASTS

TIP:
Add some raisins, cinnamon or cocoa powder to the pancake batter for extra flavor.

1. VANILLA PROTEIN PANCAKES

Serves: 8   ⏱ **Cook:** 15 min.   ⏱ **Total:** 20 min.

INGREDIENTS:

150 g. | 1½ cups
Pea protein isolate

100 g. | ½ cup
Whole wheat flour

375 ml. | 1½ cups
Almond milk
(can be substituted
with water)

8 g. | 2 tsp.
Baking powder

20 ml. | 2 tsp.
Vanilla extract

OPTIONAL TOPPINGS:

Walnuts

Blueberries
(fresh or frozen)

Shredded coconut

ALLERGENS

Whole wheat flour (gluten)
(can be substituted
with chickpea flour)

METHOD:

1. Add all ingredients to a blender and blend until smooth, scraping down the sides of the blender to prevent any lumps if necessary.

2. Put a non-stick frying pan over medium heat.

3. Pour a large tablespoon of batter into the frying pan and bake until the edges are dry and bubbles form in the pancake.

4. Flip the pancake and bake the other side until it's lightly browned.

5. Repeat the process for the remaining pancake batter.

6. Serve the pancakes with the optional toppings and enjoy!

7. Store the pancakes in an airtight container in the fridge and consume within 3 days. Alternatively, store in the freezer for a maximum of 30 days and thaw at room temperature. Use a microwave or non-stick frying pan to reheat the pancakes before serving.

2. CHOCO BERRY PUDDING

INGREDIENTS:

3 bananas
(peeled)

60 g. | 2 scoops
Organic soy isolate
(chocolate flavor)

32 g. | ¼ cup
Flaxseeds

140 g. | 1 cup
Mixed berries
(fresh or frozen)

720 ml. | 3 cups
Water

OPTIONAL TOPPINGS:

Mint leaves

Cocoa powder

Coconut flakes

ALLERGENS

Soy protein
(can be substituted
with pea protein)

METHOD:

1. Add all the ingredients to a blender and blend until smooth.
   Alternatively, blend the berries and 2 tablespoons of flaxseeds first and half fill two glasses, bowls or Mason jars with the berry mix.

2. *Blend the remaining ingredients afterwards, and top the berry mix with the banana protein mix.*

3. Serve with the optional toppings and enjoy!

4. Store the pudding in an airtight container in the fridge, and consume within 2 days. Alternatively, store in the freezer for a maximum of 60 days and thaw at room temperature.

3. MANGO CHOCO PROTEIN PUDDING

INGREDIENTS:

250 g. | 2 cups
Mango cubes
(fresh or frozen)

1 banana
(peeled)

60 g. | 2 scoops
Organic soy isolate
(chocolate flavor)

30 g. | ¼ cup
Flaxseeds

720 ml. | 3 cups
Water

OPTIONAL TOPPINGS:

Blueberries

Cocoa powder

Kiwi slices

ALLERGENS

Soy protein
(can be substituted
with pea protein)

METHOD:

1. Add all the ingredients to a blender and blend until smooth.

2. *Alternatively, blend the banana, soy isolate, 2 tablespoons of flaxseeds and the water first and divide half of the mixture between two glasses, bowls or Mason jars.*

3. *Scoop out the remaining banana mix into a glass or bowl and set it aside for now.*

4. *Blend the mango with the remaining flaxseeds.*

5. *Divide the mango purée between the two glasses, bowls or Mason jars, and top with the remaining banana mix.*

6. Serve with the optional toppings and enjoy!

Store the pudding in an airtight container in the fridge, and consume within 2 days. Alternatively, store in the freezer for a maximum of 60 days and thaw at room temperature.

4. CHOCOLATE AVOCADO SMOOTHIE

INGREDIENTS:

225 g. | 1 cup
Spinach
(fresh or frozen)

60 g. | 2 scoops
Organic soy isolate
(chocolate flavor)

2 bananas
(peeled)

1 small Hass avocado
(peeled, stoned)

30 g. | ¼ cup
Flaxseeds

720 ml. | 3 cups
Water

OPTIONAL TOPPINGS:

Lemon slices

Mint leaves

ALLERGENS

Soy protein
(can be substituted
with pea protein)

METHOD:

1. Add all the ingredients to a blender and blend until smooth.

2. Serve with the optional toppings and enjoy!

3. Store the smoothie in an airtight container in the fridge, and consume within 2 days. Alternatively, store in the freezer for a maximum of 60 days and thaw at room temperature.

5. GINGERBREAD SMOOTHIE

INGREDIENTS:

60 y. | 2 scoops
Organic soy isolate
(chocolate flavor)

2 bananas
(peeled)

1 medium Hass avocado
(peeled, stoned)

16 g. | 2 tbsp.
Chia seeds

20 g. | 2 tbsp.
5-spice powder

720 ml. | 3 cups
Water

OPTIONAL TOPPINGS:

Blueberries

Shredded coconut

Cocoa powder

ALLERGENS

Soy protein
(can be substituted
with pea protein)

METHOD:

1. Add all the ingredients to a blender and blend until smooth.

2. Serve with the optional toppings and enjoy!

3. Store the pudding in an airtight container in the fridge, and consume within 2 days. Alternatively, store in the freezer for a maximum of 60 days and thaw at room temperature.

6. APPLE CINNAMON OATS BOWL

Serves: 2   ○ **Cook:** 5 min.   ○ **Total:** 10 min.

INGREDIENTS:

1 green apple
(skinned, cored)

90 g. | 1 cup
Instant oats

25 g. | 1 scoop
Organic soy isolate
(chocolate flavor)

40 g. | ¼ cup
Raisins

10 g. | 1 tbsp.
Cinnamon

480 ml. | 2 cups
Water

OPTIONAL TOPPINGS:

Apple slices

Raisins

Cinnamon

ALLERGENS

Soy protein
(can be substituted
with pea protein)

METHOD:

1. Cut the cored and skinned apple into tiny pieces and add them to a saucepan.

2. Add the water and oats to the saucepan and put it over medium heat.

3. Bring to a boil and cook the oats for about 5 minutes.

4. Turn the heat off, add the soy isolate, raisins and cinnamon, then stir thoroughly until everything is well combined.

5. Serve warm with the optional toppings and enjoy!

6. Store the oats in an airtight container in the fridge, and consume within 2 days. Alternatively, store in the freezer for a maximum of 60 days and thaw at room temperature.

7. PALEO POWER BREAD

Serves: 8   🕐 **Cook:** 20 min.   🕐 **Total:** 30 min.

INGREDIENTS:

140 g. | 1 cup
Almonds

7 dates
(pitted)

120 g. | 1 cup
Pumpkin seeds

130 g. | 1 cup
Sunflower seeds

130 g. | 1 cup
Flaxseeds

60 ml. | ¼ cup
Water

ALLERGENS

Almonds
(can be substituted
with hemp seeds)

METHOD:

1. Preheat the oven to 257°F/125°C and line a bread tin with parchment paper.

2. Add all the ingredients to a food processor and blend into a chunky dough.

   Alternatively, chop the dates into tiny bits, crush the almonds and add them to a large bowl with the remaining ingredients and knead it into a chunky dough by hand.

3. Add the mixture to the bread tin, spread it out from edge to edge and smooth out the top with a tablespoon.

4. Transfer the bread tin to the oven and bake for 20 minutes.

5. Take the bread out of the oven and allow it to cool down completely. (If you don't, the bread will fall apart when you cut a slice!)

6. Store the bread in an airtight container and consume within 4 days. Alternatively, store in the freezer for a maximum of 90 days and thaw at room temperature.

TIP:

Serve with avocado for a healthy and balanced breakfast.

8. BUCKWHEAT PROTEIN BREAD

Serves: 6   🕐 **Cook:** 40 min.   🕐 **Total:** 50 min.

INGREDIENTS:

100 g. | 1 cup
Buckwheat flour

50 g. | ½ cup
Pea protein

40 g. | ¼ cup
Chia seeds

40 g. | ¼ cup
Raisins

30 g. | 3-inch piece
Ginger
(minced)

480 ml. | 2 cups
Water

METHOD:

1. Preheat the oven to 375°F/190°C and line a small loaf pan with parchment paper.

2. Add all the ingredients except the raisins to a food processor and blend into a smooth and sticky dough.

3. *Alternatively, add all ingredients to a large bowl and mix into a dough using a handheld mixer.*

4. Add the raisins to the dough in the food processor container and stir to distribute them evenly, using a spatula.

5. Transfer the dough to the bread tin, spread it from edge to edge and smooth out the top with a tablespoon.

6. Transfer the bread tin to the oven and bake for 40 minutes.

7. Take the bread out of the oven and allow it to cool down completely. (If you don't, the bread will fall apart when you cut a slice!)

8. Store the bread in an airtight container and consume within 4 days. Alternatively, store in the freezer for a maximum of 90 days and thaw at room temperature.

9. CHOCO ALMOND MOUSSE PUDDING

Serves: 2   ⏱ **Total:** 5 min.

INGREDIENTS:

480 ml. | 2 cups
Soymilk

170 g. | 1 cup
Pomegranate seeds

2 bananas
(peeled)

60 g. | 2 scoops
Organic soy isolate
(chocolate flavor)

60 g. | ¼ cup
Almond butter

240 ml. | 1 cup
Water
(optional when using
blender)

OPTIONAL TOPPINGS:

Blueberries

Shredded coconut

ALLERGENS

Soy protein
(can be substituted
with pea protein)
Almond butter
(can be substituted
with sunflower seed butter)

METHOD:

1. Add all the ingredients to a blender and blend until smooth.

   Alternatively, blend the bananas, soy isolate and almond butter until smooth.

2. *Add a heaped tablespoon of the almond butter mixture to 2 large glasses or Mason jars.*

3. *Add ¼ cup of soymilk and a tablespoon of pomegranate seeds to each glass or jar.*

4. *Repeat steps 3 and 4 until all of the almond mixture, pomegranate seeds and soymilk has been used.*

5. Serve with the optional toppings and enjoy!

6. Store the pudding in an airtight container in the fridge, and consume within 2 days. Alternatively, store in the freezer for a maximum of 60 days and thaw at room temperature.

10. CHOCOLATE CHERRY OATS BOWL

Serves: 2   🕐 Cook: 5 min.   🕐 Total: 10 min.

INGREDIENTS:

110 g. | ½ cup
Cherries
(fresh or frozen)

2 tangerines

90 g. | 1 cup
Instant oats

30 g. | 1 scoop
Soy protein isolate
(chocolate flavor)

25 g. | ¼ cup
Almond flakes

480 ml. | 2 cups
Water

OPTIONAL TOPPINGS:

Crushed dark chocolate

Mint leaves

Cinnamon

ALLERGENS

Soy protein
(can be substituted
with pea protein)

METHOD:

1. Add the water and oats to the saucepan and put it over medium heat.

2. Bring to a boil and cook the oats for about 5 minutes.

3. Turn the heat off and add the soy isolate while stirring thoroughly until everything is well combined.

4. Peel and section the tangerines.

5. Transfer the protein oats to a bowl, then garnish with the almond flakes, tangerines and cherries.

6. Serve the oats bowl warm with the optional toppings and enjoy!

7. Store the oats in an airtight container in the fridge, and consume within 2 days. Alternatively, store in the freezer for a maximum of 60 days and thaw at room temperature.

II. ORANGE SUNRISE SMOOTHIE

Serves: 2   🕐 **Total:** 5 min.

INGREDIENTS:

225 g. | 1 cup
Pineapple chunks

2 oranges
(peeled and quartered)

60 g. | 2 scoops
Pea protein

30 g. | ¼ cup
Flaxseeds

480 ml. | 2 cups
Water

OPTIONAL TOPPINGS:

Cocoa powder

Mint leaves

Shredded coconut

METHOD:

1. Add all the ingredients to a blender and blend until smooth.

2. Serve with the optional toppings and enjoy!

3. Store the smoothie in an airtight container in the fridge, and consume within 2 days. Alternatively, store in the freezer for a maximum of 60 days and thaw at room temperature.

12. STRAWBERRY BANANA SMOOTHIE

Serves: 2   ⏱ **Total:** *5 min.*

INGREDIENTS:

150 g. | 1 cup
Strawberries
(fresh or frozen)

225 g. | 1 cup
Spinach
(fresh or frozen)

2 bananas

60 g. | 2 scoops
Pea protein

30 g. | ¼ cup
Flaxseeds

480 ml. | 2 cups
Water

OPTIONAL TOPPINGS:

Mint leaves

Shredded coconut

Cocoa powder

METHOD:

1. Add all the ingredients to a blender and blend until smooth.

2. Serve with the optional toppings and enjoy!

3. Store the smoothie in an airtight container in the fridge, and consume within 2 days. Alternatively, store in the freezer for a maximum of 60 days and thaw at room temperature.

MEALS

NOTE: Generic store-bought burger spices work perfectly, but a variety of seasonings and spice mixes like Cajun seasoning or Provencal herbs are good fit.

1. TEMPEH SPLIT PEA BURGERS

Serves: 8 | 🕐 **Cook:** 25 min. | 🕐 **Total:** 30 min.

INGREDIENTS:

600 g. | 3 cups
Split peas
(cooked or canned)

400 g. | 1 **14-oz** pack
Tempeh

125 ml. | ½ cup
Full-fat coconut milk

30 g. | 3 tbsp.
Ground flaxseeds

50 g. | 3 tbsp.
Burger spices

OPTIONAL TOPPINGS:

Spicy tahini dressing
(See recipe on page 27)

Sauerkraut

Red onion

ALLERGENS

Tempeh (soy)
(can be substituted
with chickpea tempeh)

METHOD:

1. When using dry split peas, soak and cook 1 cup (200 g.) of dry split peas according to the method on page 20 if necessary.

2. Preheat the oven to 350°F/175°C and line a baking sheet with parchment paper.

3. Add the tempeh to a food processor and blend into a chunky mixture, scraping down the sides of the food processor to prevent any lumps if necessary.

4. Add the split peas, ground flaxseed and spices to the food processor and slowly process it along with the tempeh while pouring in the coconut milk to form a chunky mixture.

   Alternatively, crumble the tempeh by hand in a large bowl, add the remaining ingredients and mash everything into a chunky mixture.

5. Put all of the mixture on the baking sheet, and flatten it into a 1-inch thick square. Cut the square into 8 patties and if preferred, shape each patty into a circle before baking.

6. Bake the patties for 15 minutes. Then take the baking sheet out of the oven, flip the patties and bake for another 10 minutes.

7. Take the patties out of the oven once the crust is crispy and browned and let them cool down for about a minute.

8. Serve the patties with the optional toppings and whole wheat buns, and enjoy!

9. Store the patties in an airtight container in the fridge, and consume within 3 days. Alternatively, store each patty separately in the freezer, using Ziploc bags, for a maximum of 60 days and thaw at room temperature. Use a microwave, toaster oven, or frying pan to reheat the patties.

Calories: 236   Carbs: 18 g.   Fat: 9.5 g.   Protein: 18.3 g.   Fiber: 10 g.   Sugar: 2.2 g.   *per serving*

2. CRISPY MARINATED TEMPEH

Serves: 2   ○ **Cook:** 25 min.   ○ **Total:** 2 hr. 30 min.

INGREDIENTS:

*400 g. | 1 **14-oz** pack*
Tempeh
(cubed)

60 ml. | ¼ cup
Low-sodium soy sauce

60 ml. | ¼ cup
Lemon juice

30 g. | 4-inch piece
Ginger
(minced)

4 cloves
Garlic
(minced)

OPTIONAL TOPPINGS:

Spicy satay sauce
(See recipe on page 33)

Sauerkraut

Shredded coconut

ALLERGENS

Tempeh (soy)
(can be substituted
with chickpea tempeh)
Soy sauce (gluten)
(can be substituted with gluten-
free tamari or coconut aminos)

METHOD:

1. Put the tempeh cubes in an airtight with all the other ingredients (except the optional toppings).

2. Close the lid and shake well until the tempeh cubes are evenly covered with the marinade.

3. Put the airtight container in the fridge for at least 2 hours, and up to 24 hours, to make sure the tempeh is thoroughly marinated. (24 hours of marinating yields the best results.)

4. Preheat the oven to 375°F/190°C and line a baking sheet with parchment paper.

5. Transfer the tempeh cubes onto the baking sheet and bake for about 25 minutes or until the tempeh is browned and crispy.

6. Serve the tempeh with the optional toppings and enjoy!

7. Store the tempeh in an airtight container in the fridge, and consume within 3 days. Alternatively, store it in the freezer for a maximum of 60 days and thaw at room temperature. The tempeh can be eaten cold or reheated in a toaster oven or a non-stick frying pan.

Calories: 431   Carbs: 10.5 g.   Fat: 19.4 g.   Protein: 47.9 g.   Fiber: 11.8 g.   Sugar: 0.1 g.   per serving

TIP: Use a teriyaki sauce instead of the BBQ sauce for marinating the tempeh and top the tempeh with peanut butter before serving.

NOTE: The whole wheat buns are not included in the nutrition information because the nutrition information can vary a lot.

3. BBQ-LT SANDWICH

Serves: 2   ⏱ Cook: 15 min.   ⏱ Total: 1 hr. 20 min..

INGREDIENTS:

200 g. | 1 7-oz pack
Tempeh
(thinly sliced)

120 ml.
BBQ sauce
(See recipe on page 29)

2 large tomatoes
(sliced)

4 leaves
Lettuce

4 whole wheat buns

OPTIONAL TOPPINGS:

Guacamole
(See recipe on page 36)

BBQ sauce
(See recipe on page 29)

Red onion

ALLERGENS

Tempeh (soy)
(can be substituted
with chickpea tempeh)
Whole wheat buns (gluten)
(can be substituted
with gluten-free buns)

METHOD:

1. Add the tempeh slices and the BBQ sauce to an airtight container.

2. Close the airtight container, shake well and put it in the fridge, allowing the tempeh to marinate for 1 hour, up to 12 hours.

3. Preheat the oven to 375°F/190°C and line a baking sheet with parchment paper.

4. Transfer the tempeh slices onto the baking sheet and bake for about 15 minutes or until the tempeh is browned and crispy.

5. Bake the buns with the tempeh for the last 5 minutes if you want crispy and browned bread.

6. Spread the optional guacamole on the bottom half of each bun and add a lettuce leaf on top,

7. Put a quarter of the BBQ tempeh slices on top of the lettuce on each bun and top with 2 slices of tomato on each bun.

8. Cover with the top halves of the buns, serve the sandwiches right away and enjoy!

9. Store the BBQ tempeh in an airtight container in the fridge, and consume within 2 days. Alternatively, store in the freezer for a maximum of 60 days and thaw at room temperature. The tempeh can be served cold or reheated in a toaster oven or a non-stick frying pan.

TIP:

Cook the quinoa
in vegetable stock
for a more flavorful
dish.

4. MANGO SATAY TEMPEH BOWL

Serves: 4   🕐 **Cook:** 30 min.   🕐 **Total:** 40 min.

INGREDIENTS:

170 g. | 1 cup
Black beans
(cooked or canned)

90 g. | ½ cup
Quinoa
(dry)

*400 g. | 1 **14-oz** pack*
Tempeh
(sliced)

260 g. | 1 cup
Peanut butter

125 g. | 1 cup
Mango cubes
(frozen or fresh)

OPTIONAL TOPPINGS:

Chili flakes

Shredded coconut

ALLERGENS

Tempeh (soy)
(can be substituted
with chickpea tempeh)

METHOD:

1. When using dry beans, soak and cook ⅓ cup (56 g.) of dry black beans according to the method on page 20 if necessary and cook the quinoa according to the package instructions.

2. Blend the mango into a smooth puree using a blender or food processor or blender, and set it aside.

3. Add the tempeh slices and the peanut butter to an airtight container.

4. Close the lid and shake well until the tempeh slices are evenly covered with the peanut butter.

5. Preheat the oven to 375°F/190°C and line a baking sheet with parchment paper.

6. Transfer the peanut butter tempeh slices onto the baking sheet and bake for about 15 minutes or until the tempeh is browned and crispy.

7. Divide the black beans, quinoa, mango puree and tempeh slices between two bowls, serve with the optional toppings and enjoy!

8. Store the mango tempeh bowl in an airtight container in the fridge, and consume within 2 days. Alternatively, store in the freezer for a maximum of 30 days and thaw at room temperature. Serve cold (reheating the tempeh and beans is not necessary.)

TIP:

Change up the spice mix for Provencal herbs or Adobo seasoning for a tasty variation.

Use cauliflower rice for a low carb dish.

5. FRIED RICE WITH TOFU SCRAMBLE

INGREDIENTS:

400 g. | 4 cups
Quick-cooking brown rice
(cooked)

200 g. | 1 cup
Green peas
(cooked or canned)

200 g. | 1 7-oz pack
Extra-firm tofu
(scrambled)

50 g. | 1 cup
Carrots
(julienned)

40 g. | ¼ cup
Curry spices

240 ml. | 1 cup
Water

OPTIONAL TOPPINGS:

Lemon slices

Sauerkraut

Fresh cilantro

ALLERGENS

Tofu (soy)
(can be substituted
with hempfu)

METHOD:

1. Cook 1½ cup of brown rice according to the package instructions.

2. Put a large non-stick frying pan over medium heat and add ½ cup of water and the tofu scramble.

3. Add the curry spices and cook for about 5 minutes, stirring occasionally to prevent the tofu from sticking to the pan, until the tofu is well heated and most of the water has evaporated.

4. Add the carrots, rice, and green peas along with the remaining ½ cup water and stir-fry for another 5 minutes or until the water has evaporated.

5. Turn off the heat, divide the fried rice between 2 bowls, serve with the optional toppings and enjoy!

6. Store the fried rice in an airtight container in the fridge, and consume within 3 days. Alternatively, store in the freezer for a maximum of 30 days and thaw at room temperature. Reheat the fried rice in a non-stick frying pan or microwave.

6. SOY MINCE NOODLE BOWL

Serves: 2   🕐 **Cook:** 15 min.   🕐 **Total:** 25 min.

INGREDIENTS:

100 g. | 2 packs
Brown rice noodles

200 g. | 1 7-oz pack
Textured soy mince

2 yellow onions
(minced)

4 cloves
Garlic
(minced)

60 ml. | ¼ cup
Low-sodium soy sauce

360 ml. | 1½ cups
Water

OPTIONAL TOPPINGS:

Sauerkraut

Chili flakes

Roasted sesame seeds

ALLERGENS

Soy mince
(can be substituted
with pea-based mince)
Soy sauce (gluten)
(can be substituted with gluten-
free tamari or coconut aminos)

METHOD:

1. Cook the noodles according to the package instructions, drain the excess water with a strainer and set aside.

2. Put a medium pot over medium heat and add ½ cup of water, the soy sauce, minced onion and garlic.

3. Add the soy mince and cook for about 5 minutes, stirring occasionally to prevent the soy mince from sticking to the pan, until the mince has cooked, and half of the water has evaporated.

4. Add the remaining water and bring to a boil while stirring occasionally.

5. Turn off the heat, add the noodles and stir well until everything is evenly mixed.

6. Divide the noodles and mince between 2 bowls, serve with the optional toppings and enjoy!

7. Store the noodles in an airtight container in the fridge, and consume within 2 days. Alternatively, store in the freezer for a maximum of 30 days and thaw at room temperature. Reheat the noodles in a non-stick frying pan or microwave.

Calories: 226   Carbs: 26.3 g.   Fat: 0.7 g.   Protein: 25.3 g.   Fiber: 9.4 g.   Sugar: 10 g.   *per serving*

7. SWEET POTATO TACOS

Serves: 6 tacos   ○ **Cook:** 5 min.   ○ **Total:** 35 min.

INGREDIENTS:

340 g. | 2 cups
Black beans
(cooked or canned)

200 g. | 1 7-oz pack
Textured soy mince

200 g.
3 small sweet potatoes
(cubed)

6 whole wheat taco shells

40 g. | ¼ cup
Mexican chorizo seasoning

240 ml. | 1 cup
Water

OPTIONAL TOPPINGS:

Red onion

Lemon slices

Jalapeno slices

ALLERGENS

Soy mince
(can be substituted
with pea-based mince)
Whole wheat Tacos (gluten)
(can be substituted
with corn tacos)

METHOD:

1. When using dry beans, soak and cook 1½ cup (113 g.) of dry black beans according to the method on page 20 if necessary.

2. Cook the sweet potato cubes, covered with water, in a medium pot over medium-high heat for about 15 minutes or until they're soft. Drain the excess water and set the potatoes aside for now

3. Put a non-stick deep frying pan over medium-high heat and add the soy mince, black beans, chorizo seasoning and the cup of water.

4. Stir continuously until everything is cooked, then add the cooked sweet potato cubes.

5. Turn the heat off and stir occasionally for about 5 minutes until everything is heated through.

6. Divide the sweet potato mixture over 6 taco shells, serve with the optional toppings and enjoy!

7. Store the sweet potato mixture in an airtight container in the fridge, and consume within 3 days. Alternatively, store in the freezer for a maximum of 30 days and thaw at room temperature. Use a microwave, toaster oven, or non-stick frying pan to reheat the sweet potato mixture.

TIP:
Use vitamin D enhanced button mushrooms if they're locally available.

They are usually labeled "UV-treated" or "high in vitamin D."

8. MARINATED MUSHROOM SCRAMBLE

Serves: 4   ⏱ Cook: 15 min.   ⏱ Total: 1 hr. 10 min.

INGREDIENTS:

200 g. | 2 cups
Button mushrooms

400 g. | 1 **14-oz** pack
Extra-firm tofu
(scrambled)

2 medium yellow onions
(thinly sliced)

60 ml. | ¼ cup
Low-sodium soy sauce

120 g. | ½ cup
Tahini

120 ml. | ½ cup
Water

OPTIONAL TOPPINGS:

Black pepper

Parsley

Lemon slices

ALLERGENS

Tofu (soy)
(can be substituted
with hempfu)
Soy sauce (gluten)
(can be substituted with gluten-free
tamari or soy-free coconut aminos)

METHOD:

1. Add the mushrooms, tofu scramble and soy sauce to an airtight container.

2. Close the lid and shake well until everything is evenly covered with soy sauce.

3. Put the container in the fridge and leave to marinate for at least an hour, or up to 12 hours.

4. Put a large non-stick frying pan over medium heat and add the water and tofu mushroom mixture to the pan.

5. Add the onion slices and cook for about 15 minutes, stirring occasionally with a spatula to prevent the tofu from sticking to the pan, until the mushrooms are cooked and most of the water has evaporated.

6. Turn off the heat and divide the tofu mushroom scramble between 2 bowls.

7. Top the bowls with the tahini, serve with the optional toppings and enjoy!

8. Store the tofu mushroom scramble in an airtight container in the fridge, and consume within 2 days. Alternatively, store in the freezer for a maximum of 30 days and thaw at room temperature. Reheat the tofu mushroom scramble in a non-stick frying pan or microwave.

9. MAC 'N' MINCE

Serves: 4   ⏱ Cook: 10 min.   ⏱ Total: 30 min.

INGREDIENTS:

200 g. | 2 cups
Whole wheat macaroni

200 g. | 7-oz pack
Textured soy mince

120 g. | ½ cup
Tahini

40 g. | ¼ cup
Nutritional yeast

20 g. | 2 tbsp.
Lemon garlic pepper seasoning

120 ml. | ½ cup
Water

20 g. | 2 tbsp.
Optional: turmeric
(for food coloring)

OPTIONAL TOPPINGS:

Sundried tomatoes

Crispy onions

ALLERGENS

Soy mince
(can be substituted
with pea-based mince)
Whole wheat macaroni (gluten)
(can be substituted with lentil pasta)

METHOD:

1. Cook the macaroni according to package instructions and set it aside afterwards.

2. Put a non-stick deep frying pan over medium high heat and add the soy mince with the ¼ cup of water.

3. Stir fry the soy mince until it is cooked and most of the water has evaporated.

4. Add the tahini, ¼ cup of water, nutritional yeast, lemon garlic pepper seasoning and the optional turmeric to the soy mince.

5. Cook a little longer, stirring continuously, until everything is well combined.

6. Add the cooked macaroni to the pan with soy mince and stir thoroughly until the mac 'n' mince is mixed well.

7. Divide the mac 'n' mince between two plates, serve with the optional toppings and enjoy!

8. Store the mac 'n' mince in an airtight container in the fridge, and consume within 3 days. Alternatively, store it in the freezer for a maximum of 30 days and thaw at room temperature. Use a microwave, toaster oven, or frying pan to reheat the mac 'n' mince.

NOTE: If you're using canned lentils, make sure to drain all of the excess liquid.

TIP: Cook the chickpeas in vegetable stock for a more flavorful dish.

10. MOROCCAN CHICKPEA ROLLS

Serves: 4 (approx. 16 rolls)   **Cook:** 25 min.   **Total:** 35 min.

INGREDIENTS:

1000 g. | 5 cups
Chickpeas
(cooked or canned)

60 ml. | ¼ cup
Full-fat coconut milk

40 g. | ¼ cup
Ras El Hanout

OPTIONAL TOPPINGS:

Lemon mint tahini cream
(See recipe on page 35)

Pomegranate ginger sauce

BBQ sauce
(See recipe on page 29)

METHOD:

1. When using dry chickpeas, soak and cook 1½ cup (330 g.) of dry chickpeas according to the method on page 20 if necessary.

2. Preheat the oven to 350°F/175°C and line a baking sheet with parchment paper.

3. Add the chickpeas and spices to the food processor and slowly process it while pouring in the coconut milk to form a chunky mixture.

   Alternatively, mash the chickpeas and spices together in a large bowl, then add the coconut milk and knead everything into a chunky mixture.

4. Grab a handful of chickpea mixture and knead into a log shape, about 4 inches (10 cm) long and 2 inch (5 cm) thick.

5. Repeat with the remaining mixture until you have 16 rolls in total.

6. Place the chickpea rolls on the baking sheet, then bake for 15 minutes.

7. Take the baking sheet out of the oven, turn the rolls over and bake for another 10 minutes.

8. Take the rolls out of the oven once they're browned and crispy on the outside.

9. Let them cool down for about a minute.

10. Serve the rolls with the optional toppings and enjoy!

11. Store the rolls in an airtight container in the fridge, and consume within 3 days. Alternatively, store the rolls in the freezer, using Ziploc bags, for a maximum of 60 days and thaw at room temperature. Enjoy the rolls cold or use a microwave, toaster oven, or frying pan to reheat them.

TIP:

Use cauliflower rice for a low carb dish.

Cook the brown rice in vegetable stock for a more flavorful dish.

NOTE:
If smoked tofu is not locally available, add a few drops of liquid smoke during step 3.

11. SMOKY CAJUN BOWL

Serves: 4   ⏲ Cook: 25 min.   🕑 Total: 45 min.

INGREDIENTS:

340 g. | 2 cups
Black beans
(cooked or canned)

190 g. | 1 cup
Quick-cooking brown rice
(dry)

200 g. | 1 7-oz pack
Smoked tofu
(cubed)

360 g. | 2 cups
Tomato cubes
(canned or fresh)

10 g. | 1 tbsp.
Salt-free Cajun spices

60 ml. | ¼ cup
Optional: water
(if using fresh tomatoes)

OPTIONAL TOPPINGS:

Jalapeno slices

Fresh cilantro

Avocado slices

ALLERGENS

Smoked tofu (soy)
(can be substituted with hempfu)

METHOD:

1. When using dry beans, soak and cook ⅔ cup (113 g.) of dry black beans according to the method on page 20 if necessary. Cook the brown rice according to the package instructions.

2. Put a non-stick deep frying pan over medium-high heat and add the tofu cubes, tomato cubes and the optional ¼ cup of water.

3. Stir occasionally until everything is cooked, then add the black beans, cooked brown rice and Cajun spices.

4. Turn the heat off and stir occasionally for about 5 minutes until everything is heated through.

5. Divide the smoky Cajun beans and rice between 4 bowls, serve with the optional toppings and enjoy!

6. Store the smoky Cajun beans and rice in an airtight container in the fridge, and consume within 3 days. Alternatively, store in the freezer for a maximum of 30 days and thaw at room temperature. Use a microwave, toaster oven, or non-stick frying pan to reheat the smoky Cajun beans and rice.

NOTE:

The whole wheat buns are not included in the nutrition information because the nutrition information can vary a lot.

12. SLOPPY CAJUN BURGERS

Serves: 4   ○ **Cook:** 5 min.   ○ **Total:** 30 min.

INGREDIENTS:

170 g. | 1 cup
Black beans
(cooked or canned)

200 g. | 1 **7-oz** pack
Textured soy mince

180 g. | 1 cup
Tomato cubes
(canned or fresh)

40 g. | ¼ cup
Salt-free Cajun spices

4 whole wheat buns

OPTIONAL TOPPINGS:

Dill pickle slices

Tahini

Red onion

ALLERGENS

Soy mince
(can be substituted
with pea-based mince)
Whole wheat buns (gluten)
(can be substituted
with gluten-free buns)

METHOD:

1. When using dry beans, soak and cook ⅓ cup (56 g.) of dry black beans according to the method on page 20.

2. Put a non-stick deep frying pan over medium high heat and add the soy mince, and the tomato cubes.

3. Let it cook for about 3 minutes, stirring occasionally with a spatula, until everything is cooked.

4. Add the black beans and Cajun spices and let it cook for another 2 minutes while stirring.

5. Turn off the heat and divide the bottom halves of the buns between 2 plates.

6. Transfer a quarter of the sloppy Cajun mix onto each of the bun halves and add the optional toppings.

7. Cover each burger with the other bun half, serve right away and enjoy!

8. Store the sloppy Cajun mix in an airtight container in the fridge, and consume within 2 days. Alternatively, store in the freezer for a maximum of 60 days and thaw at room temperature. The sloppy Cajun mix can be served cold or reheated in a microwave or a saucepan.

TIP:

Mix up flavors with a Provencal herb mix, Italian herbs or even Ras El Hanout spices.

Use zucchini noodles for a low carb dish.

13. SPAGHETTI BOLOGNESE

Serves: 4   ⏲ Cook: 5 min.   ⏲ Total: 30 min.

INGREDIENTS:

200 g. | 2 cups
Whole wheat spaghetti
(dry)

*200 g. | 1 **7-oz** pack*
Textured soy mince

3 cloves
Garlic
(minced)

180 g. | 1 cup
Tomato cubes
(canned or fresh)

7g. | ¼ cup
Basil
(fresh or dried)

OPTIONAL TOPPINGS:

Cashew cream cheese
(See recipe on page 25)

Green olives

Black pepper

ALLERGENS

Soy mince
(can be substituted
with pea-based mince)
Whole wheat pasta (gluten)
(can be substituted with lentil pasta)

METHOD:

1. Cook the spaghetti according to package instructions, drain the water with a strainer and set it aside afterwards.

2. Put a non-stick deep frying pan over medium high heat and add the soy mince, minced garlic, tomato cubes and basil.

3. Let it cook for about 2 minutes, stirring occasionally with a spatula, until everything is cooked.

4. Turn off the heat, the divide the spaghetti between 2 plates and add half of the sauce on top of the spaghetti on each plate.

5. Serve with the optional toppings and enjoy!

6. Store the spaghetti and sauce in an airtight container in the fridge, and consume within 3 days. Alternatively, store in the freezer for a maximum of 30 days and thaw at room temperature. Use a microwave or a saucepan to reheat the spaghetti and sauce.

TIP: Substitute the Mexican chorizo seasoning for a Cajun spice mix and add ¼ cup smoked chipotles.

NOTE: Don't use canned black beans because they're too mushy for a solid burger patty!

Alternatively add a binder such as flour if you don't have any other options.

14. BLACK BEAN QUINOA BURGERS

Serves: 4 (approx. 8 patties)   ⏱ **Cook:** 35 min.   ⏱ **Total:** 45 min.

INGREDIENTS:

180 g. | 1 cup
Quinoa
(dry)

340 g. | 2 cups
Black beans
(cooked)

40 g. | ¼ cup
**Mexican chorizo
seasoning**

OPTIONAL TOPPINGS:

BBQ sauce
(See recipe on page 29)

Guacamole
(See recipe on page 36)

Red onion

METHOD:

1. When using dry beans, soak and cook ⅔ cup (113 g.) of dry black beans according to the method on page 20 if necessary. Cook the quinoa according to the package instructions.

2. Preheat the oven to 375°F/190°C and line a baking sheet with parchment paper.

3. Add the cooked black beans, quinoa and spices to a food processor and blend into a chunky mixture, scraping down the sides of the food processor to prevent any lumps if necessary.

   Alternatively, add the ingredients to a large bowl and mash them into a chunky mixture.

4. Put all of the mixture on the baking sheet, flatten it into a 1-inch-thick square, cut the square into 8 patties and if preferred, shape each patty into a circle before baking.

5. Bake the patties for 10 minutes, then take the baking sheet out of the oven, flip the patties and bake for another 10 minutes.

6. Take the patties out of the oven once the crust is crispy and browned and let them cool down for about a minute.

7. Serve the patties with the optional toppings, whole wheat buns and enjoy!

8. Store the patties in an airtight container in the fridge, and consume within 3 days. Alternatively, store each patty separately in the freezer, using Ziploc bags, for a maximum of 60 days and thaw at room temperature. Use a microwave, toaster oven, or frying pan to reheat the patties.

TIP: Cook the chickpeas in vegetable stock for a more flavorful dish.

NOTE: If you're using canned chickpeas, make sure to drain all of the excess liquid.

15. TOMATO CURRY FRITTERS

Serves: 8 (approx. 24 fritters)   ⏱ **Cook:** 16 min.   ⏱ **Total:** 30 min.

INGREDIENTS:

1000 g. | 5 cups
Chickpeas
(cooked or canned)

2 sweet onions
(diced)

12 sundried tomatoes

3 cloves
Garlic
(minced)

40 g. | ¼ cup
Curry spices

OPTIONAL TOPPINGS:

Lemon mint tahini cream
(See recipe on page 35)

Mexican Salsa
(See recipe on page 31)

Guacamole
(See recipe on page 36)

METHOD:

1. When using dry chickpeas, soak and cook 1½ cup (330 g.) of dry chickpeas according to the method on page 20 if necessary.

2. Preheat the oven to 375°F/190°C and line a baking sheet with parchment paper.

3. Add the chickpeas, onion, sundried tomatoes, garlic and spices to the food processor and process them into a chunky mixture.

   Alternatively, mince the sundried tomatoes and mash them together with the chickpeas and other ingredients in a large bowl, then knead them into a chunky mixture.

4. Take a tablespoon of chickpea mixture and knead into a 2-inch-thick (5cm) disc, then place on the baking sheet. Repeat with the rest of the mixture until you have around 24 fritters.

5. Bake the fritters for 8 minutes, then take the baking sheet out of the oven, turn the fritters over and bake for another 8 minutes.

6. Take the fritters out of the oven once they're browned and crispy on the outside. Let them cool down for about a minute.

7. Serve the fritters with the optional toppings and enjoy!

8. Store the fritters in an airtight container in the fridge, and consume within 3 days. Alternatively, store in the freezer, using Ziploc bags, for a maximum of 60 days and thaw at room temperature. Enjoy the fritters cold or use a microwave, toaster oven, or frying pan to reheat them.

NOTE:

If smoked tofu is not locally available, add a few drops of liquid smoke during step 5.

16. SMOKED TOFU AND BEANS BOWL

Serves: 2   ⏱ **Cook:** 15 min.   ⏱ **Total:** 25 min.

INGREDIENTS:

170 g. | 1 cup
Black beans
(cooked or canned)

*200 g. | 1 **7-oz** pack*
Smoked tofu
(cubed)

1 small Hass avocado
(peeled, stoned)

180 g. | 2 cups
Sweet corn
(cooked or canned)

60 g. | ¼ cup
Lemon juice

OPTIONAL TOPPINGS:

Jalapeno slices

Fresh cilantro

Red onion

ALLERGENS

Smoked tofu (soy)
(can be substituted
with hempfu)

METHOD:

1. When using dry beans, soak and cook ⅓ cup (56 g.) of dry black beans according to the method on page 20.

2. Preheat the oven to 350°F/175°C and line a baking sheet with parchment paper.

3. Put the tofu cubes on the baking sheet and bake for 10 minutes or until the tofu is slightly browned and dry.

4. Take the tofu cubes out of the oven and let them cool down for about 5 minutes.

5. Cut one half of the peeled avocado into cubes and the other half into slices.

6. Toss the 'tofu cubes, black beans, avocado cubes, and corn in a large salad bowl and stir well using a spatula until everything is evenly mixed.

7. Divide between two bowls if necessary, then drizzle 2 tablespoons of lemon juice on top of each bowl, garnish with the avocado slices, serve with the optional toppings and enjoy!

8. Store the tofu and beans in an airtight container in the fridge, and consume within 2 days. Alternatively, store in the freezer for a maximum of 60 days and thaw at room temperature. The tofu and beans can be served cold.

TIP:

Cook the chickpeas in vegetable stock for a more flavorful dish.

Serve with basmati rice or vegan naan bread.

17. CHANA MASALA

Serves: 2   ⏱ Cook: 25 min.   ⏱ Total: 30 min.

INGREDIENTS:

400 g. | 2 cups
Chickpeas
(cooked or canned)

180 g. | 1 cup
Tomato cubes
(canned or fresh)

2 medium onions
(minced)

20 g. | 2 tbsp.
Curry spices

60 ml. | ¼ cup
Water

OPTIONAL TOPPINGS:

Fresh chili slices

Lime juice

Shredded coconut

METHOD:

1. When using dry chickpeas, soak and cook ⅔ cup (133 g.) of dry chickpeas to the method on page 20.

2. Put a large pot over medium heat, then add the tomato cubes, onions, and the water.

3. Cook for a few minutes, stirring occasionally, until everything is cooked, then add the curry spices and stir thoroughly.

4. Add the chickpeas, and stir thoroughly to make sure that everything is well mixed.

5. Cook for a couple more minutes, stirring occasionally, then lower the heat to a simmer.

6. Let the curry simmer for about 20 minutes while stirring occasionally.

7. Turn the heat off and let the curry cool down for a minute.

8. Divide curry between 2 bowls, garnish with the optional toppings, serve and enjoy!

9. Store the curry in an airtight container in the fridge, and consume within 2 days. Alternatively, store in the freezer for a maximum of 30 days and thaw at room temperature. Reheat the curry in the microwave or a saucepan.

TIP:

Use a vegan barbeque sauce instead of the teriyaki sauce for marinating the tempeh.

18. TERIYAKI TEMPEH LETTUCE WRAPS

Serves: 4　　🕐 Cook: 15 min.　　🕐 Total: 25 min.

INGREDIENTS:

400 g. | 1 14-oz pack
Tempeh

60 ml. | ¼ cup
Teriyaki sauce

1 small red onion
(minced)

50 g. | 1 cup
Carrots
(julienned)

4 large leaves
Lettuce

OPTIONAL TOPPINGS:

Chili flakes

Lime juice

Peanut butter

ALLERGENS

Tempeh (soy)
(can be substituted
with chickpea tempeh)
Teriyaki sauce (soy)
(can be substituted
with BBQ sauce)

METHOD:

1. Cut the tempeh into small cubes, put them into an airtight container and add the teriyaki sauce.

2. Close the airtight container, shake well and put it in the fridge, allowing the tempeh to marinate for at least 1 hour, up to 12 hours.

3. Preheat the oven to 375°F/190°C and line a baking sheet with parchment paper.

4. Transfer the tempeh cubes onto the baking sheet and bake for about 15 minutes or until the tempeh is browned and crispy.

5. Lay out 4 large lettuce leaves, add a quarter or the tempeh to each leaf, and top it with the minced red onion and julienned carrots.

6. Serve with the optional toppings and enjoy!

7. Store the tempeh in an airtight container in the fridge, and consume within 2 days. Alternatively, store it in the freezer for a maximum of 60 days and thaw at room temperature. The tempeh can be served cold or reheated in a toaster oven or a non-stick frying pan.

TIP:
Cook the lentils in vegetable stock for a more flavorful dish.

Serve with basmati rice or vegan naan bread.

19. RED LENTIL DAHL

Serves: 2   ⏱ Cook: 15 min.   ⏱ Total: 30 min.

INGREDIENTS:

400 g. | 2 cups
Red lentils
(cooked or canned)

180 g. | 1 cup
Tomato cubes
(canned or fresh)

20 g. | 2 tbsp.
Curry spices

20 g. | ¼ cup
Shredded coconut

60 ml. | ¼ cup
Water

OPTIONAL TOPPINGS:

Lime juice

Cherry tomatoes

Nigella seeds

METHOD:

1. When using dry lentils, soak and cook ⅔ cup (133 g.) of dry lentils according to the method on page 20 if necessary.

2. Put a large pot over medium heat, and add the tomato cubes, shredded coconut, and the water.

3. Cook for a few minutes, stirring occasionally, until everything is cooked, then add the curry spices and stir thoroughly.

4. Add the lentils, stir thoroughly making sure everything is well mixed.

5. Cook for a couple more minutes, stirring occasionally, until everything is cooked, then lower the heat to a simmer.

6. Let the dahl simmer for about 15 minutes while stirring occasionally.

7. Turn the heat off and let the dahl cool down for a minute.

8. Divide the lentil dahl between 2 bowls, garnish with the optional toppings, serve and enjoy!

9. Store the dahl in an airtight container in the fridge, and consume within 2 days. Alternatively, store in the freezer for a maximum of 30 days and thaw at room temperature. Reheat the dahl in the microwave or a saucepan.

TIP:

Use cauliflower rice for a low carb dish.

Cook the brown rice in vegetable stock for a more flavorful dish.

Serves: 3   ⏱ **Cook:** 30 min.   ⏱ **Total:** 40 min.

INGREDIENTS:

190 g. | 1 cup
Quick-cooking brown rice
(cooked)

200 g. | 1 7-oz pack
Extra-firm tofu
(cubed)

350 g. | 2 cups
Broccoli florets

180 g. | 1 cup
Tomato cubes

15 g. | ¼ cup
Provencal herbs

30 ml. | 2 tbsp.
Water

OPTIONAL TOPPINGS:

Basil

Sundried tomatoes

Black pepper

ALLERGENS

Tofu (soy)
(can be substituted
with hempfu)

METHOD:

1. Cook the brown rice according to the package instructions.

2. Put a medium pot filled halfway with water over high heat, add the broccoli florets and let them cook for about 5 minutes.

3. Put a non-stick deep frying pan over medium-high heat and add the tofu cubes, tomato cubes, Provencal herbs and water.

4. Let it cook for about 10 minutes while stirring occasionally.

5. Continue to cook, stirring continuously, until everything is cooked, then add the broccoli florets and stir again to mix everything.

6. Turn the heat off and let the rice mixture cool down for a minute.

7. Divide the rice and tofu with broccoli between 2 plates, garnish with the optional toppings and enjoy!

8. Store the broccoli tofu in an airtight container in the fridge, and consume within 3 days. Alternatively, store in the freezer for a maximum of 30 days and thaw at room temperature. The broccoli tofu can be eaten cold or reheated in a saucepan or a microwave.

21. SWEET POTATO & BROCCOLI BOWL

Serves: 2   ⏱ Cook: 18 min.   ⏱ Total: 35 min.

INGREDIENTS:

250 g.
4 sweet potatoes
(cubed)

200 g. | 1 7-oz pack
Smoked tofu
(cubed)

350 g. | 2 cups
Broccoli florets

60 ml. | ¼ cup
Teriyaki sauce

70 g. | ¼ cup
Peanut butter

120 ml. | ½ cup
Water

OPTIONAL TOPPINGS:

Chili flakes

Shredded coconut

Roasted sesame seeds

ALLERGENS

Smoked tofu (soy)
*(can be substituted
with hempfu)*

METHOD:

1. Cook the sweet potato cubes, covered with water, in a medium pot over medium-high heat for about 10 minutes.

2. Add the broccoli florets, and cook for another 3 minutes.

3. Take the pot off the heat, drain the excess water from the broccoli and sweet potatoes and set aside for now.

4. Put a non-stick deep frying pan over medium-high heat and add the teriyaki sauce, the water and tofu cubes.

5. Keep stirring continuously until everything is cooked, then add the broccoli florets and sweet potato cubes to the frying pan.

6. Cook for about 5 minutes while stirring occasionally.

7. Turn the heat off, leave to cool down for a minute, then drain the excess water.

8. Divide between 2 plates, drizzle half of the peanut butter on top of each plate with the optional toppings and enjoy!

9. Store in an airtight container in the fridge, and consume within 3 days. Alternatively, store in the freezer for a maximum of 30 days and thaw at room temperature. The bowl can be eaten cold or reheated in a saucepan or a microwave.

22. RAS EL HANOUT PROTEIN BOWL

INGREDIENTS:

200 g. | 1 cup
Chickpeas
(cooked or canned)

45 g. | ¼ cup
Quinoa
(dry)

130 g. | ⅔ cup
Green lentils
(dry)

720 ml. | 3 cups
Vegetable stock

20 g. | 2 tbsp.
Ras El Hanout

OPTIONAL TOPPINGS:

Raisins

Parsley

Tahini

METHOD:

1. When using dry chickpeas, soak and cook ⅓ cup (66 g.) of dry chickpeas according to the method on page 20.

2. Put a large pot over medium-high heat and add the vegetable stock and the lentils to the pot.

3. Bring the water to a boil, then turn the heat down to medium.

4. Cook the lentils for about 15 minutes without covering the pot. Stir occasionally and remove any foam produced by the lentils.

5. Add the quinoa and Ras el Hanout spices, then cook for another 15 minutes, stirring occasionally.

6. Add the chickpeas and stir well, then bring the heat down to a simmer and leave to simmer for about 5 minutes.

7. Turn the heat off and let the mixture cool down for a minute.

8. Divide between 2 bowls, garnish with the optional toppings, serve and enjoy!

9. Store in an airtight container in the fridge, and consume within 2 days. Alternatively, store in the freezer, for a maximum of 30 days and thaw at room temperature. The bowl can be served cold or reheated in a saucepan or a microwave.

23. MEXICAN QUINOA BOWL

Serves: 2   ⏱ Cook: 25 min.   ⏱ Total: 35 min.

INGREDIENTS:

200 g. | 1 cup
Chickpeas
(cooked or canned)

170 g. | 1 cup
Black beans
(cooked or canned)

90 g. | ½ cup
Quinoa
(dry)

480 ml. | 2 cups
Vegetable stock

20 g. | 2 tbsp.
**Mexican chorizo
seasoning**

OPTIONAL TOPPINGS:

Lime Juice

Fresh cilantro

Avocado slices

METHOD:

1. When using dry chickpeas and beans, soak and cook ⅓ cup (66 g.) of dry chickpeas and black beans (56 g.) according to the method on page 20.

2. Put a large pot over medium-high heat and add the vegetable stock to the pot along with the quinoa.

3. Bring to a boil, then turn the heat down to medium.

4. Cook the quinoa for about 15 minutes, without covering the pot, and stir occasionally.

5. Add the Mexican chorizo seasoning, black beans and chickpeas, and cook for another 7 minutes, stirring occasionally.

6. Turn the heat off and let it cool down for a minute.

7. Divide between 2 bowls, garnish with the optional toppings, serve and enjoy!

8. Store in an airtight container in the fridge, and consume within 2 days. Alternatively, store in the freezer for a maximum of 30 days and thaw at room temperature. The bowl can be served cold or reheated in a saucepan or a microwave.

24. CREAMY ASPARAGUS & SWEET POTATOES

Serves: 2   ⏱ **Cook:** 25 min.   ⏱ **Total:** 35 min.

INGREDIENTS:

250 g.
4 sweet potatoes

200 g. | **7-oz** *pack*
Smoked tofu
(cubed)

8 asparagus spears

60 ml. | ¼ cup
Lemon juice

60 g. | ¼ cup
Tahini

60 ml. | ¼ cup
Water

OPTIONAL TOPPINGS:

Black pepper

Parsley

ALLERGENS

Smoked tofu (soy)
(can be substituted
with hempfu)

METHOD:

1. Preheat the oven to 425°F/220°C and line a baking sheet with parchment paper.

2. Cook the sweet potato cubes, covered with water, in a medium pot over medium-high heat for about 15 minutes or until they're soft.

3. Take the pot off the heat, drain the excess water from the sweet potato cubes and set aside for now.

4. Put the asparagus spears and tofu cubes on a baking tray.

5. Roast them for about 10 minutes or until the asparagus spears are soft.

6. Whisk the tahini and lemon juice together in a bowl into a thinner and smooth dressing, adding more water if necessary. *Alternatively, put the tahini, lemon juice and garlic in a lidded container and shake, adding more water if you want a thinner and less creamy dressing.*

7. Divide the sweet potatoes, asparagus and tofu cubes between 2 plates, drizzle half of the tahini dressing on top of each plate with the optional toppings and enjoy!

8. Store in an airtight container in the fridge, and consume within 3 days. Alternatively, store in the freezer for a maximum of 30 days and thaw at room temperature. The asparagus and sweet potatoes can be eaten cold or reheated in a saucepan or a microwave.

TIP:
If you're using dry lentils, cook them in vegetable stock for a more flavorful patty.

NOTE: Generic store-bought burger spices work perfectly, but a variety of spice mixes like Cajun or Adobo spices fit as well.

If you're using canned lentils, make sure to drain all of the excess liquid.

25. SPICY LENTIL BURGERS

Serves: *4*   ⏱ **Cook:** *25 min.*   ⏱ **Total:** *40 min.*

INGREDIENTS:

400 g. | 2 cups
Green lentils
(cooked or canned)

140 g. | 1 cup
Almonds

3 dates
(pitted)

2 cloves
Garlic

40 g. | 4 tbsp.
Burger spices

OPTIONAL TOPPINGS:

BBQ sauce
(See recipe on page 29)

Guacamole
(See recipe on page 36)

Sauerkraut

METHOD:

1. When using dry lentils, soak and cook ⅔ cup (133 g.) of dry lentils according to the method on page 20.

2. Preheat the oven to 350°F/175°C and line a baking sheet with parchment paper.

3. Add all of the ingredients to a food processor and blend into a chunky mixture, scrape down the sides of the food processor to prevent any lumps if necessary.

   Alternatively, crush the almonds, mince the garlic, add all of the ingredients to a large bowl and mash them into a chunky mixture.

4. Put all of the mixture on the baking sheet, flatten it into a 1-inch thick square, cut the square into 8 patties and if preferred, shape each patty into a 1-inch thick disk before baking.

5. Bake the patties for 15 minutes, then take the baking sheet out of the oven, flip the patties and bake for another 10 minutes.

6. Take the patties out of the oven once the crust is crispy and browned, then let them cool down for about a minute.

7. Serve the patties with the optional toppings, whole wheat buns and enjoy!

8. Store the patties in an airtight container in the fridge, and consume within 3 days. Alternatively, store each patty separately in the freezer, using Ziploc bags, for a maximum of 60 days and thaw at room temperature. Use a microwave, toaster oven, or frying pan to reheat the patties.

TIP:
If you're using dry lentils, cook them in vegetable stock for a more flavorful dish.

26. RED LENTIL PASTA

Serves: 4   🕐 **Cook:** 15 min.   🕐 **Total:** 30 min.

INGREDIENTS:

300 g. | 1½ cup
Red lentils
(cooked or canned)

150 g. | 1½ cup
Whole wheat pasta
(dry)

20 g. | 2 tbsp.
Rosemary
(fresh or dried)

150 g. | ½ cup
Pistachios
(shelled)

60 ml. | ¼ cup
Lemon juice

60 ml. | ¼ cup
Water

OPTIONAL TOPPINGS:

Black pepper

Black olives

ALLERGENS

Whole wheat pasta (gluten)
(can be substituted
with lentil pasta)

METHOD:

1. When using dry lentils, soak and cook ½ cup (100 g.) of dry lentils according to the method on page 20 if necessary.

2. Cook the pasta according to package instructions, drain the water with a strainer and set the pasta aside afterwards.

3. When using fresh rosemary, remove the stem and chop the rosemary leaves into tiny bits.

4. Put a non-stick deep frying pan over medium-high heat and add lentils, rosemary, water, half of the pistachios and half of the lemon juice.

5. Let it cook for about 5 minutes, stirring occasionally with a spatula, until everything is cooked and most of the liquid has evaporated.

6. Turn off the heat and let the pasta cool down a bit.

7. Crush the remaining pistachios and divide the pasta and lentils between 2 plates.

8. Drizzle with remaining lemon juice and garnish with the crushed pistachios.

9. Serve the pasta with the optional toppings and enjoy!

10. Store the pasta in an airtight container in the fridge, and consume within 3 days. Alternatively, store in the freezer, using Ziploc bags, for a maximum of 60 days and thaw at room temperature. Enjoy the pasta cold, or use a microwave, toaster oven, or frying pan to reheat it.

TIP:

Use vitamin D enhanced button mushrooms if they're locally available.

They are usually labeled "UV-treated" or "high in vitamin D."

27. BLACK BEAN MUSHROOM BURGERS

Serves: 4 (approx. 8 patties)   🕒 **Cook:** 25 min.   🕒 **Total:** 45 min.

INGREDIENTS:

510 g. | 3 cups
Black beans
(cooked)

150 g. | 2 cups
Button mushrooms
(sliced)

1 medium onion
(quartered)

2 cloves
Garlic

60 ml. | ¼ cup
Low-sodium soy sauce

OPTIONAL TOPPINGS:

BBQ sauce
(See recipe on page 29)

Spicy satay sauce
(See recipe on page 33)

Mexican salsa
(See recipe on page 31)

ALLERGENS

Soy sauce
(can be substituted
with coconut aminos)
Soy sauce (gluten)
(can be substituted with gluten-
free tamari or coconut aminos)

METHOD:

1. When using dry beans, soak and cook 1 cup (170 g.) of dry black beans according to the method on page 20 if necessary.

2. Preheat the oven to 350°F/175°C and line a baking sheet with parchment paper.

3. Add all of the ingredients to a food processor and blend into a chunky mixture, scraping own the sides of the food processor to prevent any lumps if necessary.

   Alternatively, add the ingredients to a large bowl and mash them into a chunky mixture.

4. Put all of the mixture on the baking sheet and flatten it into a 1-inch thick square, cut the square into 8 patties and if preferred, shape each patty into a 1-inch thick disk before baking.

5. Bake the patties for 15 minutes, then take the baking sheet out of the oven, flip the patties and bake for another 10 minutes.

6. Take the patties out of the oven once the crust is crispy and browned, then let them cool down for about a minute.

7. Serve the patties with the optional toppings, whole wheat buns and enjoy!

8. Store the patties in an airtight container in the fridge, and consume within 3 days. Alternatively, store each patty separately in the freezer, using Ziploc bags, for a maximum of 60 days and thaw at room temperature. Use a microwave, toaster oven, or frying pan to reheat the patties.

28. BLACK PEPPER TEMPEH STIR-FRY

Serves: 4   ⓧ Cook: 20 min.   ⓧ Total: 80 min.

INGREDIENTS:

*400 g. | 1 **14-oz** pack*
Tempeh
(thinly sliced)

60 ml. | ¼ cup
Low-sodium soy sauce

2 medium onions
(minced)

3 cloves
Garlic
(minced)

20 g. | 2 tbsp.
Black pepper

120 ml. | ½ cup
Water

OPTIONAL TOPPINGS:

Sauerkraut

Roasted sesame seeds

Shredded coconut

ALLERGENS

Tempeh (soy)
(can be substituted
with chickpea tempeh)
Soy sauce (gluten)
(can be substituted with gluten-
free tamari or coconut aminos)

METHOD:

1. Cut the tempeh into thin slices, put them into an airtight container and add the soy sauce.

2. Close the airtight container, shake well and put it in the fridge, allowing the tempeh to marinate for at least 1 hour, or up to 12 hours.

3. Put a non-stick deep frying pan over medium-high heat and add the minced onions, minced garlic and the water.

4. Stir continuously until everything is cooked, then add the tempeh slices.

5. Let it cook for about 20 minutes while stirring occasionally.

6. Turn the heat off, leave to cool down for a minute and drain the excess water if necessary.

7. Divide between 2 plates, garnish with the optional toppings and enjoy!

8. Store the tempeh stir-fry in an airtight container in the fridge, and consume within 3 days. Alternatively, store in the freezer for a maximum of 30 days and thaw at room temperature. The tempeh stir-fry can be eaten cold or reheated in a saucepan or a microwave.

NOTE:
If you're using canned lentils, make sure to drain all of the excess liquid.

TIP:
If you're using dry lentils, cook them in vegetable stock for a more flavorful dish.

29. MEXICAN CHORIZO LENTIL LOAF

Serves: 8   ⏱ **Cook:** 40 min.   ⏱ **Total:** 50 min.

INGREDIENTS:

800 g. | 4 cups
Green lentils
(cooked or canned)

30 g. | ¼ cup
Flaxseeds

90 g. | ½ cup
Tomato cubes
(canned or fresh)

90 g. | 1 cup
Sweet corn
(cooked or canned)

40 g. | 4 tbsp.
**Mexican chorizo
seasoning**

OPTIONAL TOPPINGS:

Lime juice

Cherry Tomatoes

Guacamole
(See recipe on page 36)

METHOD:

1. When using dry lentils, soak and cook 1⅓ cup (266 g.) of dry lentils according to the method on page 20.

2. Preheat the oven to 350°F/175°C and line a loaf pan with parchment paper.

3. Add all the ingredients to a food processor and blend into a chunky mixture.

   Alternatively, add all ingredients to a large bowl and mix into a dough using a handheld mixer or potato masher.

1. Transfer the mixture to the loaf pan lined with parchment paper, spread it out from edge to edge and smooth out the top with a tablespoon.

2. Transfer the loaf pan to the oven and bake for 40 minutes.

3. Take the loaf out of the oven and allow it to cool down completely so that it doesn't fall apart when cutting a slice!

4. Garnish the desired amount of servings with the optional toppings, serve and enjoy!

5. Store the lentil loaf in an airtight container and consume within 4 days. Alternatively, store in the freezer for a maximum of 90 days and thaw at room temperature.

NOTE:
If you're using canned lentils, make sure to drain all of the excess liquid.

TIP:

Mix up flavors with a Provencal herb mix, Cajun spice mix or even Ras El Hanout spices.

If you're using dry lentils, cook them in vegetable stock for more flavorful lentil balls.

30. LENTIL BALLS PASTA

Serves: 4 (approx. 12 balls)   🕐 **Cook:** 18 min.   🕐 **Total:** 35 min.

INGREDIENTS:

300 g. | 1½ cup
Green lentils
(cooked or canned)

150 g. | 1½ cup
Whole wheat pasta
(dry)

10 sundried tomatoes

180 g. | 1 cup
Tomato cubes
(canned or fresh)

40 g. | 4 tbsp.
Italian herbs

60 ml. | ¼ cup
Water

OPTIONAL TOPPINGS:

Basil

Cashew Cream Cheese
(See recipe on page 25)

ALLERGENS

Whole wheat pasta (gluten)
(can be substituted
with lentil pasta)

METHOD:

1. When using dry lentils, soak and cook ½ cup (100 g.) of dry lentils according to the method on page 20 if necessary.

2. Preheat the oven to 350°F/175°C and line a baking sheet with parchment paper.

3. Chop 8 of the sundried tomatoes into tiny bits.

4. Using a potato masher, mash the lentils, sundried tomato bits, and 2 tablespoons (20 grams) Italian herbs together in a large bowl and knead them into a chunky mixture.

   Alternatively, knead everything by hand into a chunky mixture.

5. Grab a handful of lentil mixture and knead it into a 2-inch (5 cm) ball. Repeat the process until all of the lentil mixture is used.

6. Place the lentil balls on the baking sheet and bake for 10 minutes, then take the baking sheet out of the oven, turn the balls over and bake for another 8 minutes.

7. Cook the pasta according to package instructions, drain the water with a strainer and set the pasta aside afterwards.

8. Take the balls out of the oven once they're browned and crispy on the outside, then let them cool down for about a minute.

9. Put a non-stick deep frying pan over medium-high heat and add the tomato cubes and the remaining Italian herbs.

10. Chop the remaining 2 sundried tomatoes into bits and add them to the sauce.

11. Let it cook for about 2 minutes, stirring occasionally with a spatula, until everything is cooked.

12. Turn off the heat, divide the pasta between 2 plates, and top each one with half of the sauce and lentil balls.

13. Serve the pasta with the optional toppings and enjoy!

14. Store the lentil balls in an airtight container in the fridge, and consume within 3 days. Alternatively, store the balls in the freezer, using Ziploc bags, for a maximum of 60 days and thaw at room temperature. Enjoy the balls cold, or use a microwave, toaster oven, or frying pan to reheat them.

31. CHORIZO CHICKPEA BOWL

Serves: 4   Cook: 10 min.   Total: 20 min.

INGREDIENTS:

400 g. | 2 cups
Chickpeas
(cooked or canned)

225 g. | 1 cup
Spinach
(fresh or frozen)

40 g. | ¼ cup
Raisins

50 g. | ½ cup
Raw cashews
(unsalted)

20 g. | 2 tbsp.
**Mexican chorizo
seasoning**

120 ml. | ½ cup
Water

OPTIONAL TOPPINGS:

Raisins

Parsley

Lime juice

ALLERGENS

Cashews
(can be substituted
with sunflower seeds)

METHOD:

1. When using dry chickpeas, soak and cook ⅔ cup (133 g.) of dry chickpeas according to the method on page 20.

2. Put a non-stick deep frying pan over medium-high heat and add the spinach, chorizo seasoning and the water.

3. Stir continuously until everything is cooked, then add the chickpeas and cashew nuts. Make sure to stir again to mix everything.

4. Let it cook for about 10 minutes while stirring occasionally.

5. Turn the heat off, then add the raisins, stir well and drain the excess water.

6. Divide between 2 bowls, garnish with the optional toppings, serve and enjoy!

7. Store the chorizo chickpeas in an airtight container in the fridge, and consume within 2 days. Alternatively, store in the freezer for a maximum of 30 days and thaw at room temperature. The chorizo chickpeas can be eaten cold or reheated in a saucepan or a microwave.

1. LENTIL RICE SOUP

INGREDIENTS:

60 g. | ⅓ cup
Quick-cooking brown rice
(dry)

130 g. | ⅔ cup
Green lentils
(dry)

180 g. | 1 cup
Tomato cubes
(canned or fresh)

720 ml. | 3 cups
Vegetable stock

60 g. | ¼ cup
Tahini

OPTIONAL TOPPINGS:

Fresh chili slices

Fresh cilantro

Green peppercorns

METHOD:

1. Put a large pot over medium-high heat and add the vegetable stock along with the green lentils.

2. Bring the stock to a boil and turn the heat down to medium.

3. Cook the lentils for about 15 minutes, without covering the pot. From time to time, remove any foam produced by the lentils and give the pot a stir.

4. Add the brown rice and bring the heat down to a simmer, then cover the pot with a lid and let it simmer for another 10 minutes.

5. Add the tomato cubes and tahini, stir well and let it simmer for another 5 minutes.

6. Turn the heat off and let the soup cool down for 5 minutes.

7. Divide between two bowls, serve with the optional toppings and enjoy!

8. Store the soup in an airtight container in the fridge, and consume within 2 days. Alternatively, store in the freezer for a maximum of 60 days and thaw at room temperature. The soup can be reheated in a pot or the microwave.

NOTE:

If smoked tofu is not locally available, add a few drops of liquid smoke during step 5.

2. SPLIT PEA SOUP

INGREDIENTS:

440 g. | 2 cups
Split peas
(dry)

200 g. | **7-oz** pack
Smoked tofu
(cubed)

1200 ml. | 5 cups
Vegetable stock

2 small onions
(minced)

4 carrots
(sliced)

OPTIONAL TOPPINGS:

Parsley

Black pepper

Nigella seeds

ALLERGENS

Smoked tofu (soy)
(can be substituted
with hempfu)

METHOD:

1. Put a large pot over medium-high heat, then add the vegetable stock and the split peas.

2. Bring the stock to a boil and turn the heat down to medium.

3. Cook the split peas for about 40 minutes and don't cover the pot.

4. Remove the foam produced by the peas and stir occasionally.

5. Add the smoked tofu cubes, carrots and onions to the pot, then bring the heat down to a simmer, cover the pot with a lid, let it simmer for another 20 minutes and make sure to stir occasionally.

6. Turn the heat off and let the soup cool down for 5 minutes.

7. Divide the soup between two bowls, serve with the optional toppings and enjoy!

8. Store the soup in an airtight container in the fridge, and consume within 2 days. Alternatively, store in the freezer for a maximum of 60 days and thaw at room temperature. The soup can be reheated in a pot or the microwave.

3. TEMPEH CHILI

Serves: 4   ⏱ **Cook:** 40 min.   ⏱ **Total:** 1 hr. 50 min.

INGREDIENTS:

400 g. | 2 cups
Pinto beans
(cooked or canned)

200 g. | 7-oz pack
Tempeh

360 g. | 2 cups
Tomato cubes
(canned or fresh)

180 g. | 2 cups
Sweet corn
(cooked or canned)

60 g. | 6 tbsp.
Mexican chili spices

720 ml. | 3 cups
Water

OPTIONAL TOPPINGS:

Jalapeno slices

Fresh cilantro

Lime juice

ALLERGENS

Tempeh (soy)
(can be substituted
with chickpea tempeh)

METHOD:

1. When using dry beans, soak and cook ⅔ cup (133 g.) of dry pinto beans according to the method on page 20.

2. Cut the tempeh into small cubes, put them into an airtight container and add 2 tablespoons of the Mexican chili spices.

3. Close the airtight container, shake well and put it in the fridge, allowing the tempeh to marinate for at least 1 hour, and up to 12 hours.

4. Put a large pot over medium-high heat and add the water, tempeh cubes and the pinto beans.

5. Bring the stock to a boil, and let it cook for about 15 minutes.

6. Turn the heat down to a simmer and add the tomato cubes, corn and the remaining Mexican spices to the pot.

7. Make sure to stir well, then let it simmer for another 20 minutes.

8. Turn the heat off and let the soup cool down for 5 minutes.

9. Divide between two bowls, serve with the optional toppings and enjoy!

10. Store the soup in an airtight container in the fridge, and consume within 2 days. Alternatively, store in the freezer for a maximum of 60 days and thaw at room temperature. The soup can be reheated in a pot or the microwave.

4. BLACK BEAN SOUP

Serves: 4   ⏱ Cook: 15 min.   ⏱ Total: 30 min.

INGREDIENTS:

510 g. | 3 cups
Black beans
(cooked or canned)

180 g. | 1 cup
Tomato cubes
(canned or fresh)

960 ml. | 4 cups
Vegetable stock

90 g. | 1 cup
Sweet corn
(cooked or canned)

4 carrots
(sliced)

OPTIONAL TOPPINGS:

Jalapeno slices

Fresh cilantro

Lemon slices

METHOD:

1. When using dry beans, soak and cook 1 cup (170 g.) of dry black beans according to the method on page 20.

2. Put a large pot over medium-high heat and add the vegetable stock and the black beans.

3. Bring the stock to a boil then lower the heat down to a simmer.

4. Add the tomato cubes, corn and carrot slices to the pot, making sure to stir well, then let it simmer for another 5 minutes.

5. Turn the heat off and let the soup cool down for 5 minutes.

6. Divide between two bowls, serve with the optional toppings and enjoy!

7. Store the soup in an airtight container in the fridge, and consume within 2 days. Alternatively, store in the freezer for a maximum of 60 days and thaw at room temperature. The soup can be reheated in a pot or the microwave.

NOTE:
If smoked tofu is not locally available, add a few drops of liquid smoke during step 4.

5. SWEET POTATO STEW

Serves: 4   🕐 **Cook:** 1 hr. 5 min.   🕐 **Total:** 1 hr. 15 min.

INGREDIENTS:

220 g. | 1 cup
Split peas
(dry)

200 g. | 7-oz pack
Smoked tofu
(cubed)

120 g.
2 small sweet potatoes
(cubed)

60 g. | 6 tbsp.
Salt-free Cajun spices

1200 ml. | 5 cups
Water

2 stalks
Celery
(sliced)

OPTIONAL TOPPINGS:

Green peppercorns

Fresh cilantro

ALLERGENS

Smoked tofu (soy)
(can be substituted
with hempfu)

METHOD:

1. Put a large pot over medium-high heat, and add the water, split peas and 2 tablespoons of Cajun spices.

2. Bring the water to a boil, then turn the heat down to medium.

3. Cook the split peas for about 30 minutes without covering the pot and remove the foam produced by the peas and stir occasionally.

4. Add the sweet potato cubes, celery stalk slices and the rest of the Cajun spices, then bring the heat down to a simmer.

5. Cover the pot with a lid and let it simmer for another 15 minutes, stirring occasionally.

6. Add the tofu cubes to the pot, stir well and let it simmer for another 10 minutes.

7. Turn the heat off and let the soup cool down for 5 minutes.

8. Divide the soup between two bowls, serve with the optional toppings and enjoy!

9. Store the soup in an airtight container in the fridge, and consume within 2 days. Alternatively, store in the freezer for a maximum of 60 days and thaw at room temperature. The soup can be reheated in a pot or the microwave.

TIP:

Use vitamin D enhanced button mushrooms if they're locally available.

They are usually labeled "UV-treated" or "high in vitamin D."

6. LENTIL MUSHROOM SOUP

Serves: 4   ⏱ Cook: 35 min.   ⏱ Total: 45 min.

INGREDIENTS:

130 g. | ⅔ cup
Green lentils
(dry)

150 g. | 2 cups
Button mushrooms
(sliced)

1 red bell pepper

960 ml. | 4 cups
Vegetable stock

40 g. | ¼ cup
Dried thyme

OPTIONAL TOPPINGS:

Black pepper

Sundried tomatoes

METHOD:

1. Put a large pot over medium-high heat and add the vegetable stock along with the green lentils.

2. Bring the water to a boil and turn the heat down to medium.

3. Cook the lentils for about 15 minutes, without covering the pot, remove any foam produced by the lentils and stir occasionally.

4. Add the mushrooms and thyme to the pot, bring the heat down to a simmer, cover the pot with a lid and let it simmer for another 10 minutes.

5. Remove the stem, seeds and placenta of the bell pepper and dice the flesh.

6. Add the bell pepper to the pot, then make sure to stir well and let it simmer for another 5 minutes.

7. Turn the heat off and let the soup cool down for 5 minutes.

8. Divide between two bowls, serve with the optional toppings and enjoy!

9. Store the soup in an airtight container in the fridge, and consume within 2 days. Alternatively, store in the freezer for a maximum of 60 days and thaw at room temperature. The soup can be reheated in a pot or the microwave.

7. LENTIL PEPPER POT

Serves: 4   ⏱ **Cook:** 40 min.   ⏱ **Total:** 50 min.

INGREDIENTS:

130 g. | ⅔ cup
Green lentils
(dry)

180 g. | 1 cup
Tomato cubes
(canned or fresh)

1 red bell pepper

960 ml. | 4 cups
Vegetable stock

5 g. | ¼ cup
Fresh mint
(chopped)

OPTIONAL TOPPINGS:

Tahini

Sundried tomatoes

METHOD:

1. Put a large pot over medium-high heat and add the vegetable stock along with the green lentils.

2. Bring the stock to a boil then turn the heat down to medium.

3. Cook the lentils for about 15 minutes, without cover the pot, remove any foam produced by the lentils and stir occasionally.

4. Add the chopped mint leaves, bring the heat down to a simmer, cover the pot with a lid and let it simmer for another 10 minutes.

5. Remove the stem, seeds and placenta of the bell pepper and dice the flesh.

6. Add the tomato cubes and bell pepper to the pot, stir well and let it simmer for another 10 minutes.

7. Turn the heat off and let the soup cool down for 5 minutes.

8. Divide between two bowls, serve with the optional toppings and enjoy!

9. Store the soup in an airtight container in the fridge, and consume within 2 days. Alternatively, store in the freezer for a maximum of 60 days and thaw at room temperature. The soup can be reheated in a pot or the microwave.

8. PROVENCAL LENTIL SOUP

Serves: 4   ⏱ Cook: 35 min.   ⏱ Total: 45 min.

INGREDIENTS:

130 g. | ⅔ cup
Green lentils
(dry)

180 g. | 1 cup
Tomato cubes
(canned or fresh)

4 carrots
(sliced)

960 ml. | 4 cups
Vegetable stock

40 g. | ¼ cup
Provencal herbs

OPTIONAL TOPPINGS:

Black pepper

Cashew Cream Cheese
(See recipe on page 25)

Basil

METHOD:

1. Put a large pot over medium-high heat and add the vegetable stock along with the green lentils.

2. Bring the stock to a boil then turn the heat down to medium.

3. Cook the lentils for about 15 minutes, without covering the pot. Remove any foam produced by the lentils and stir occasionally.

4. Add the carrots and Provencal herbs to the pot, bring the heat down to a simmer, cover the pot with a lid and let it simmer for another 10 minutes.

5. Add the tomato cubes, making sure to stir well, then stir well and let it simmer for another 5 minutes.

6. Turn the heat off and let the soup cool down for 5 minutes.

7. Transfer the soup to a heat-safe blender container and blend until it's smooth.

8. Divide between two bowls, serve with the optional toppings and enjoy!

9. Store the soup in an airtight container in the fridge, and consume within 2 days. Alternatively, store in the freezer for a maximum of 60 days and thaw at room temperature. The soup can be reheated in a pot or the microwave.

9. LENTIL CHICKPEA STEW

Serves: 4   ⏱ **Cook:** 30 min.   ⏱ **Total:** 50 min.

INGREDIENTS:

130 g. | ⅔ cup
Green lentils
(dry)

200 g. | 1 cup
Chickpeas
(cooked or canned)

4 carrots
(sliced)

2 stalks
Celery
(sliced)

960 ml. | 4 cups
Vegetable stock

OPTIONAL TOPPINGS:

Parsley
(fresh or dried)

Black pepper

METHOD:

1. When using dry chickpeas, soak and cook ⅓ cup (66 g.) of dry chickpeas according to the method on page 20 if necessary.

2. Put a large pot over medium-high heat and add the vegetable stock along with the green lentils.

3. Bring the stock to a boil and turn the heat down to medium.

4. Cook the lentils for about 15 minutes, without covering the pot. Remove any foam produced by the lentils and stir occasionally.

5. Add the carrots and celery, bring the heat down to a simmer, cover the pot with a lid and let it simmer for another 10 minutes.

6. Turn the heat off and let the soup cool down for 5 minutes.

7. Divide between two bowls, serve with the optional toppings and enjoy!

8. Store the soup in an airtight container in the fridge and consume within 2 days. Alternatively, store in the freezer for a maximum of 60 days and thaw at room temperature. The soup can be reheated in a pot or the microwave.

10. MOROCCAN CHICKPEA SOUP

Serves: 4   ⏱ Cook: 20 min.   ⏱ Total: 30 min.

INGREDIENTS:

600 g. | 3 cups
Chickpeas
(cooked or canned)

1 medium onion
(minced)

1 clove
Garlic
(minced)

360 g. | 2 cups
Tomato cubes
(canned or fresh)

20 g. | 2 tbsp.
Ras El Hanout

480 ml. | 2 cups
Water

OPTIONAL TOPPINGS:

Lemon slices

Fresh cilantro

Cranberries

METHOD:

1. When using dry chickpeas, soak and cook 1 cup (200 g.) of dry chickpeas according to the method on page 20 if necessary.

2. Put a large pot over medium-high heat, and add the water, minced onions and garlic to the pot.

3. Bring the water to a boil then turn the heat down to medium.

4. Add the chickpeas and the Ras El Hanout spices and continue to cook, stirring occasionally.

5. After about 5 minutes bring the heat down to a simmer.

6. Add the tomato cubes, cover the pot with a lid and let it simmer for another 10 minutes.

7. Turn the heat off and let the stew cool down for 5 minutes.

8. Divide between two bowls, serve with the optional toppings and enjoy!

9. Store the soup in an airtight container in the fridge, and consume within 2 days. Alternatively, store in the freezer for a maximum of 60 days and thaw at room temperature. The stew can be reheated in a pot or the microwave.

11. CHICKPEA KALE POT

Serves: 4   ⏱ **Cook:** 15 min.   ⏱ **Total:** 25 min.

INGREDIENTS:

600 g. | 3 cups
Chickpeas
(cooked or canned)

225 g. | 1 cup
Kale
(frozen)

8 sundried tomatoes
(chopped)

50 g. | ½ cup
Raw cashews
(unsalted)

960 ml. | 4 cups
Vegetable stock

OPTIONAL TOPPINGS:

Black pepper

Fresh cilantro

Sundried tomatoes

METHOD:

1. When using dry chickpeas, soak and cook 1 cup (200 g.) of dry chickpeas according to the method on page 20 if necessary.

2. Put a large pot over medium-high heat, and add the vegetable stock and kale to the pot.

3. Bring the water to a boil and let the kale defrost while stirring occasionally.

4. Let everything cook for a minute then turn the heat down to medium.

5. Add the chickpeas, stir occasionally and after about 5 minutes bring the heat down to a simmer.

6. Add the chopped sundried tomatoes and the cashews, cover the pot with a lid and let it simmer for another 10 minutes.

7. Turn the heat off and let the soup cool down for 5 minutes.

8. Divide between two bowls, serve with the optional toppings and enjoy!

9. Store the soup in an airtight container in the fridge, and consume within 2 days. Alternatively, store in the freezer for a maximum of 60 days and thaw at room temperature. The soup can be reheated in a pot or the microwave.

SALADS

1. PROVENCAL BEANS & TOMATO SALAD

Serves: 2   ⏱ Total: 10 min.

INGREDIENTS:

400 g | 2 cups
White beans (navy beans)
(cooked or canned)

1 small red onion
(minced)

8 cherry tomatoes
(halved)

60 ml. | ¼ cup
Lemon juice

30 g. | 3 tbsp.
Provencal herbs
(dried)

OPTIONAL TOPPINGS:

Pine nuts

Black pepper

METHOD:

1. When using dry white beans, soak and cook ⅔ cup (133 g.) of dry white beans according to the method on page 20 if necessary.

2. Transfer the white beans to a large bowl, and add the minced red onion, halved cherry tomatoes, lemon juice and herbs.

3. Stir thoroughly using a spatula and make sure everything is mixed evenly.

4. Divide the white beans salad between two bowls, garnish with the optional toppings, serve and enjoy!

5. Store the salad in an airtight container in the fridge, and consume within 2 days. Alternatively, store in the freezer for a maximum of 30 days and thaw at room temperature. The salad can be served cold.

TIP:

Cook the quinoa in vegetable stock for a more flavorful salad.

2. PINEAPPLE QUINOA SALAD

Serves: 3　　　　　⏱ **Cook:** 15 min.　　　⏱ **Total:** 25 min.

INGREDIENTS:

340 g. | 2 cups
Black beans
(cooked or canned)

90 g. | ½ cup
Quinoa
(dry)

110 g. | 1 cup
Pineapple chunks
(fresh or frozen)

8 cherry tomatoes
(halved)

1 red onion
(minced)

OPTIONAL TOPPINGS:

Chili flakes

Soy sauce

Shredded coconut

METHOD:

1. When using dry beans, soak and cook ⅔ cup (113 g.) of dry black beans according to the method on page 20 if necessary. Cook the quinoa according to the package instructions.

2. Add all of the ingredients to a large bowl and mix thoroughly.

3. Divide the salad between 3 bowls, serve with the optional toppings and enjoy!

4. Store the salad in an airtight container in the fridge, and consume within 2 days. Alternatively, store in the freezer for a maximum of 30 days and thaw at room temperature. The salad can be served cold.

3. FIERY COUSCOUS SALAD

Serves: 3   ⏲ **Cook:** 5 min.   ⏲ **Total:** 10 min.

INGREDIENTS:

200 g. | 1 cup
Chickpeas
(cooked or canned)

75 g. | ½ cup
Couscous
(dry)

3 tangerines

20 g. | 2-inch piece
Ginger
(minced)

60 g. | ¼ cup
Tahini

120 ml. | ½ cup
Water

OPTIONAL TOPPINGS:

Cinnamon

Fresh mint

Raisins

ALLERGENS

Couscous
(can be substituted
with quinoa)

METHOD:

1. When using dry chickpeas, soak and cook ⅓ cup (66 g.) of dry chickpeas according to the method on page 20 if necessary. Cook the couscous according to the package instructions.

2. Meanwhile, add the tahini, minced ginger and water to a small airtight container or bowl. Whisk the tahini and ginger in the bowl into a smooth dressing, adding more water if necessary.

   Alternatively, shake the container with tahini, ginger and water until everything is thoroughly mixed, adding more water if you want a thinner and less creamy dressing.

1. Add the couscous, dressing and chickpeas to a large bowl and mix thoroughly.

2. Peel and section the tangerines and set them aside to garnish the salad.

3. Divide the salad between two bowls, garnish with the tangerines and the optional toppings, serve and enjoy!

4. Store the salad in an airtight container in the fridge, and consume within 2 days. Alternatively, store in the freezer for a maximum of 30 days and thaw at room temperature. The salad can be served cold.

TIP:

If you're using dry lentils, cook them in vegetable stock for a more flavorful dish.

4. GREEN LENTIL SALAD

Serves: 2   🕐 *Total: 10 min.*

INGREDIENTS:

400 g. | 2 cups
Green lentils
(cooked or canned)

110 g. | ½ cup
Endive
(fresh)

60 ml. | ¼ cup
Lemon juice

10 g. | 1 tbsp.
Ground black pepper

20 g. | 2 tbsp.
Oregano
(dried)

OPTIONAL TOPPINGS:

Cashew cream cheese
(See recipe on page 25)

Black pepper

METHOD:

1. When using dry lentils, soak and cook ⅔ cup (133 g.) of dry lentils according to the method on page 20 if necessary.

2. Transfer the lentils to a large bowl and add the black pepper, oregano and lemon juice.

3. Stir thoroughly using a spatula and make sure everything is mixed evenly.

4. Put the endive in a strainer, rinse well to clean it thoroughly and then drain well.

5. Divide the endive over two bowls, add half of the green lentils, garnish with the optional toppings, serve and enjoy!

6. Store the salad in an airtight container in the fridge, and consume within 2 days. Alternatively, store in the freezer for a maximum of 30 days and thaw at room temperature. The salad can be served cold.

TIP:

If you're using dry lentils, cook them in vegetable stock for a more flavorful dish.

5. MANGO LENTIL SALAD

INGREDIENTS:

400 g. | 2 cups
Red lentils
(cooked or canned)

250 g. | 2 cups
Mango cubes
(fresh or frozen)

110 g. | ½ cup
Spinach
(fresh)

8 cherry tomatoes
(halved)

5 g. | 2 tsp.
Cumin seeds

OPTIONAL TOPPINGS:

Shredded coconut

Nigella seeds

METHOD:

1. When using dry lentils, soak and cook ⅔ cup (133 g.) of dry lentils according to the method on page 20 if necessary.

2. Meanwhile, add the mango cubes and cumin to a blender and blend into a smooth puree.

3. Put the spinach in a strainer, rinse well to clean it thoroughly and then drain well.

4. Divide the spinach, tomatoes and lentils between two bowls, top with half of the mango puree and the optional toppings, serve and enjoy!

5. Store the salad in an airtight container in the fridge, and consume within 2 days. Alternatively, store in the freezer for a maximum of 30 days and thaw at room temperature. The salad can be served cold.

6. WHITE BEANS SUMMER SALAD

INGREDIENTS:

400 g. | 2 cups
White beans (navy beans)
(cooked or canned)

½ cucumber
(cubed)

8 sundried tomatoes
(minced)

4 tangerines

10 g. | 1 tbsp.
Thyme
(fresh or dried)

OPTIONAL TOPPINGS:

Black pepper

Tahini

METHOD:

1. When using dry white beans, soak and cook ⅔ cup (133 g.) of dry white beans according to the method on page 20 if necessary.

2. Transfer the white beans to a large bowl, and add the minced sundried tomatoes, cucumber cubes and thyme. If using fresh thyme, chop it finely before adding it to the bowl.

3. Stir thoroughly using a spatula and make sure everything is mixed evenly.

4. Peel and section the tangerines and set them aside to garnish the salad.

5. Divide the white beans salad between two bowls, garnish with the tangerine and the optional toppings, serve and enjoy!

6. Store the salad in an airtight container in the fridge, and consume within 2 days. Alternatively, store in the freezer for a maximum of 30 days and thaw at room temperature. The salad can be served cold.

TIP:

If you're using dry lentils, cook them in vegetable stock for a more flavorful dish.

7. LENTIL CRANBERRY SALAD

Serves: 2 ⏱ **Total:** *10 min.*

INGREDIENTS:

400 g. | 2 cups
Green lentils
(cooked or canned)

1 small red onion
(minced)

½ cucumber
(cubed)

60 ml. | ¼ cup
Lemon juice

30 g. | ¼ cup
Cranberries
(dried)

OPTIONAL TOPPINGS:

Black pepper

Tahini

METHOD:

1. When using dry lentils, soak and cook ⅔ cup (133 g.) of dry lentils according to the method on page 20 if necessary.

2. Transfer the lentils to a large bowl, and add the minced red onion, cucumber cubes, lemon juice and cranberries.

3. Stir thoroughly using a spatula and make sure everything is mixed evenly.

4. Divide the lentil salad between two bowls, garnish with the optional toppings, serve and enjoy!

5. Store the salad in an airtight container in the fridge, and consume within 2 days. Alternatively, store in the freezer for a maximum of 30 days and thaw at room temperature. The salad can be served cold.

8. PINTO SALSA BOWL

INGREDIENTS:

400 g. | 2 cups
Pinto beans
(cooked or canned)

1 small Hass avocado
(peeled, stoned, cubed)

10 cherry tomatoes
(halved)

60 ml. | ¼ cup
Lime juice

15 g. | ¼ cup
Fresh cilantro
(chopped)

OPTIONAL TOPPINGS:

Red onion

Jalapeno slices

Sweet corn

METHOD:

1. When using dry pinto beans, soak and cook ⅔ cup (133 g.) of dry pinto beans according to the method on page 20 if necessary.

2. Transfer the pinto beans to a large bowl, and add the halved cherry tomatoes, avocado cubes, and chopped cilantro.

3. Add the lime juice, stir thoroughly using a spatula and make sure everything is mixed evenly.

4. Divide the pinto salsa between two bowls, garnish with the optional toppings, serve and enjoy!

5. Store the salad in an airtight container in the fridge, and consume within 2 days. Alternatively, store in the freezer for a maximum of 30 days and thaw at room temperature. The salad can be served cold.

9. LEMON GARLIC CHICKPEAS SALAD

Serves: 2   ⏱ Total: 10 min.

INGREDIENTS:

200 g. | 1 cup
Chickpeas
(cooked or canned)

110 g. | ½ cup
Spinach
(fresh)

60 ml. | ¼ cup
Lemon juice

60 g. | ¼ cup
Tahini

1 clove
Garlic
(minced)

60 ml. | ¼ cup
Water

OPTIONAL TOPPINGS:

Fresh cilantro

Raisins

METHOD:

1. When using dry chickpeas, soak and cook ⅓ cup (66 gr.) of dry chickpeas according to the method on page 20 if necessary.

2. Meanwhile, add the tahini, minced garlic, lemon juice and water to a small airtight container or bowl.

3. Whisk the tahini, lemon juice, garlic and water in the bowl to form a thinner and smooth dressing, adding more water if necessary. *Alternatively, shake the container with tahini, lemon juice, garlic and water until everything is thoroughly mixed, adding more water if you want a thinner and less creamy dressing.*

4. Put the spinach in a strainer, rinse well to clean it thoroughly and then drain well.

5. Add the spinach and chickpeas to a large bowl and mix thoroughly.

6. Divide the salad between two bowls, garnish with the tangerines and the optional toppings, serve and enjoy!

7. Store the salad in an airtight container in the fridge, and consume within 2 days. Alternatively, store in the freezer for a maximum of 30 days and thaw at room temperature. The salad can be served cold.

10. CHICKPEA APPLE SALAD

Serves: 2   🕐 Cook: 15 min.   🕐 Total: 30 min.

INGREDIENTS:

200 g. | 1 cup
Chickpeas
(cooked or canned)

90 g. | ½ cup
Quinoa
(dry)

80 g. | ½ cup
Pomegranate seeds

60 g. | ¼ cup
Tahini

1 large apple
(skinned, cored)

OPTIONAL TOPPINGS:

Fresh mint

Black pepper

METHOD:

1. When using dry chickpeas, soak and cook ⅓ cup (66 g.) of dry chickpeas according to the method on page 20 if necessary. Cook the quinoa according to the package instructions.

2. Meanwhile, cut the skinned and cored apple into small bits and set them aside for now.

3. Add the cooked chickpeas and quinoa to a large bowl and mix.

4. Add the pomegranate seeds and apple bits to the same bowl and mix thoroughly using a spatula. Optionally leave some pomegranate seeds and apple bits for garnishing later.

5. Stir the tahini into the chickpea and quinoa salad and make sure everything is mixed well.

6. Divide the salad between two bowls, optionally garnish with the leftover pomegranate seeds, apple bits and a swirl of tahini, any of the optional toppings and enjoy!

7. Store the salad in an airtight container in the fridge, and consume within 2 days. Alternatively, store in the freezer for a maximum of 30 days and thaw at room temperature. The salad can be served cold.

SNACKS & DESSERTS

NOTE: *No blender? Mince the dates and nuts as fine as possible, knead all the ingredients by hand and add a quarter cup of water to make everything stick together.*

1. LEMON PIE BARS

Makes: 8   🕐 Cook: 15 min.   🕐 Total: 50 min.

INGREDIENTS:

200 g. | 2 cups
Cashews
(raw and unsalted)

10 dates
(pitted)

60 g. | 2 scoops
Organic pea protein

1 organic lemon

10 ml. | 1 tsp.
Vanilla extract

OPTIONAL TOPPINGS:

Coconut whipped cream
(See recipe on page 34)

Cocoa powder

Shredded coconut

ALLERGENS

Cashews
(can be substituted
with sunflower seeds)

METHOD:

1. Preheat the oven to 257°F/125°C and line a baking sheet with parchment paper.

2. Put the cashews on the baking sheet and roast them for about 10 to 15 minutes or until they're fragrant.

3. Meanwhile, cover the dates with water in a small bowl and let them sit for about 10 minutes. Drain the dates after soaking and make sure no water is left.

4. Rinse and scrub the lemon lightly to clean it.

5. Add the cashews, dates, pea protein, the whole lemon and vanilla extract to a food processor and blend into a smooth mixture.

   Alternatively, add all ingredients to a medium bowl, cover it, and process using a handheld blender.

6. Line a loaf pan with parchment paper. Add the cashew mixture to the loaf pan, spread it out and press it down firmly until it's 1-inch (2.5 cm) thick all over.

7. Put the loaf pan in the fridge for about 45 minutes, until it has firmed up.

8. Divide into 8 bars, serve cold with the optional toppings and enjoy!

9. Store the bars in an airtight container in the fridge and consume within 6 days. Alternatively, store in the freezer for a maximum of 90 days and thaw at room temperature.

NOTE: *No blender? Mince the dates and nuts as fine as possible, knead all the ingredients by hand and add a quarter cup of water to make everything stick together.*

2. COCONUT CRUMBLE BARS

Makes: 8 bars   ⏱ **Cook:** 15 min.   ⏱ **Total:** 20 min.

INGREDIENTS:

280 g. | 2 cups
Almonds
(raw and unsalted)

10 dates
(pitted)

60 g. | 2 scoops
Organic soy isolate
(chocolate flavor)

50 g. | ½ cup
Cocoa powder

50 g. | ½ cup
Shredded coconut

ALLERGENS

Soy protein
(can be substituted
with pea protein)
Almonds
(can be substituted
with sunflower seeds)

METHOD:

1. Preheat the oven to 257°F/125°C and line a baking sheet with parchment paper.

2. Put the almonds on the baking sheet and roast them for about 10 to 15 minutes or until they're fragrant.

3. Meanwhile, cover the dates with water in a small bowl and let them sit for about 10 minutes. Drain the dates after soaking and make sure no water is left.

4. Add the almonds, dates, chocolate protein and cocoa powder to a food processor and blend into a chunky mixture.

   Alternatively, add all ingredients to a medium bowl, cover it, and process using a handheld blender.

5. Line a loaf pan with parchment paper. Add the almond mixture to the loaf pan, spread it out and press it down firmly until it's 1-inch-thick (2.5 cm) all over.

6. Add the shredded coconut in an even layer on top and press it down firmly to make it stick.

7. Divide into 8 bars, serve cold and enjoy!

8. Store the bars in an airtight container in the fridge, and consume within 6 days. Alternatively, store in the freezer for a maximum of 90 days.

NOTE: Don't have a mixer? Knead all the ingredients by hand and add a quarter cup of water to make everything stick together.

3. PROTEIN MUFFINS

Makes: 8   ⏱ **Cook:** *25 min.*   ⏱ **Total:** *30 min.*

INGREDIENTS:

150 g. | 1½ cups
Pea protein isolate

100 g. | ½ cup
Whole wheat flour

375 ml. | 1½ cups
Water

40 g. | ¼ cup
Raisins

8 g. | 2 tsp.
Baking powder

20 ml. | 2 tsp.
Vanilla extract

OPTIONAL TOPPINGS:

Coconut whipped cream
(See recipe on page 34)

Cocoa powder

ALLERGENS

Whole wheat flour (gluten)
(can be substituted
with chickpea flour)

METHOD:

1. Preheat the oven to 320°F/160°C, line a muffin tray with muffin liners and set it aside.

2. Add all ingredients to a blender and blend until smooth, scraping down the sides of the blender to prevent any lumps if necessary.

   Alternatively, add all ingredients to a medium bowl, and mix it using a handheld mixer.

3. Spoon the mixture into the muffin liners until each one is about three-quarters filled.

4. Bake the muffins for 20-25 minutes, then test to see if they are done by sticking a toothpick in to see if it comes out mostly clean.

5. Take the muffins out of the oven and let them cool down completely before taking the muffin liners off.

6. Serve the muffins with the optional toppings and enjoy!

7. Store the muffins in an airtight container in the fridge and consume within 3 days. Alternatively, store in the freezer for a maximum of 30 days and thaw at room temperature.

NOTE: No blender? Mince the dates and nuts as fine as possible, knead all the ingredients by hand and add a quarter cup of water to make everything stick together.

4. CHOCO ALMOND BARS

Makes: *4 bars*　　🕐 **Cook:** *15 min.*　　🕐 **Total:** *20 min.*

INGREDIENTS:

140 g. | 1 cup
Almonds
(raw and unsalted)

5 dates
(pitted)

30 g. | 1 scoop
Organic soy isolate
(chocolate flavor)

OPTIONAL TOPPINGS:

Shredded coconut

Cocoa powder

ALLERGENS

Soy protein
(can be substituted
with pea protein)
Almonds
(can be substituted
with sunflower seeds)

METHOD:

1. Preheat the oven to 257°F/125°C and line a baking sheet with parchment paper.

2. Put the almonds on the baking sheet and roast them for about 10 to 15 minutes or until they're fragrant.

3. Meanwhile, cover the dates with water in a small bowl and let them sit for about 10 minutes. Drain the dates after soaking and make sure no water is left.

4. Take the almonds out of the oven and let them cool down for about 5 minutes.

5. Add all the ingredients to a food processor and blend into a chunky mixture.

   Alternatively, add all ingredients to a medium bowl, cover it, and process using a handheld blender.

6. Line a loaf pan with parchment paper. Add the almond mixture to the loaf pan, spread it out and press it down firmly until it is 1 inch (2.5 cm) thick all over.

7. Divide into 4 bars, serve cold with the optional toppings and enjoy!

8. Store the bars in an airtight container in the fridge and consume within 4 days. Alternatively, store in the freezer for a maximum of 90 days and thaw at room temperature.

5. OATS 'N' RAISINS COOKIES

Makes: 8   ⏱ **Cook:** 15 min.   ⏱ **Total:** 30 min.

INGREDIENTS:

90 g. | 1 cup
Instant oats

4 bananas

40 g. | ¼ cup
Raisins

60 g. | 2 scoops
Organic soy isolate
(chocolate flavor)

10 ml. | 1 tsp.
Vanilla extract

OPTIONAL TOPPINGS:

Coconut whipped cream
(See recipe on page 34)

Cocoa powder

Shredded coconut

ALLERGENS

Soy protein
(can be substituted
with pea protein)

METHOD:

1. Preheat the oven to 325°F/170°C, line a baking tray with parchment paper and set it aside.

2. Add all ingredients to a food processor and process until smooth, scraping down the sides of the container if necessary.

   Alternatively, add all ingredients to a medium bowl, cover it, and process using a handheld blender.

3. Take a tablespoon of the mixture, put it on the baking tray lined with parchment paper and press it down to form a 0.3 inch (1 cm) thick cookie. Repeat the process for the remaining cookie dough and make sure there is a bit of space between each cookie.

4. Transfer the baking tray to the oven and bake the cookies for about 15 minutes, until they have set.

5. Take the cookies out of the oven and let them cool down before serving.

6. Serve the cookies with the optional toppings and enjoy!

7. Store the cookies in an airtight container in the fridge and consume within 3 days. Alternatively, store in the freezer for a maximum of 30 days and thaw at room temperature.

6. CRISPY CAJUN TOFU

Serves: 4   🕐 Cook: 20 min.   🕐 Total: 1 hr.

INGREDIENTS:

200 g. | 1 7-oz pack
Extra-firm tofu

20 g. | 2 tbsp.
Salt-free Cajun spices

60 g. | ¼ cup
Tahini

30 ml. | 2 tbsp.
Lemon juice

1 clove
Garlic
(minced)

60 ml. | ¼ cup
Water

OPTIONAL DIPS:

Pomegranate ginger sauce
(See recipe on page 37)

BBQ sauce
(See recipe on page 29)

Spicy satay sauce
(See recipe on page 33)

ALLERGENS

Tofu (soy)
(can be substituted
with hempfu)

METHOD:

1. Drain the tofu first by slicing it into 3 or 4 slabs. Lay a few paper towels or a clean tea towel on a flat surface.

2. Put the tofu slabs side by side on the towels, cover them another tea towel or paper towel, place a cutting board on top and place heavy objects on top of the cutting board to press out any excess water. Let the tofu drain for about 15-30 minutes.

3. Cut the tofu after draining into thin slices or cubes, then transfer them to a medium bowl.

4. Add the Cajun spices and toss to cover the tofu evenly. Cover the bowl and let it marinate while preheating the oven.

5. Preheat the oven to 325°F/175°C, line a baking tray with parchment paper and arrange the marinated tofu slices onto the baking tray.

6. Bake the tofu for about 10 minutes, then remove the baking tray from the oven, flip over the tofu and bake again for about 10 minutes until they're crispy.

7. Meanwhile, add the tahini, lemon juice, minced garlic and water to a small airtight container or bowl.

8. Whisk the tahini, lemon juice and garlic in the bowl into a thinner and smooth dressing, adding more water if necessary. *Alternatively, shake the container with tahini, lemon juice and garlic until everything is thoroughly mixed. Adding more water if you want a thinner and less creamy dressing.*

9. Take the tofu out of the oven and let it cool down for about 5 minutes.

10. Serve the tofu with the tahini dressing and the optional dips and enjoy!

11. Store the tofu in an airtight container in the fridge and consume within 3 days.

NOTE: *No blender? Mince the plums and nuts as fine as possible, knead all the ingredients by hand and add a quarter cup of water to make everything stick together.*

7. HAZELNUT CHOCO PLUM BITES

Makes: 12 balls   ⏱ Total: 1 hr.

INGREDIENTS:

200 g. | 2 cups
Hazelnuts
(roasted)

8 dried plums
(pitted)

90 g. | 1 cup
Soy protein isolate
(chocolate flavor)

50 g. | ½ cup
Cocoa powder

OPTIONAL TOPPINGS:

Crushed dark chocolate

Crushed hazelnuts

ALLERGENS

Soy protein
(can be substituted
with pea protein)
Hazelnuts
(can be substituted
with sunflower seeds)

METHOD:

1. Transfer the hazelnuts, plums and soy protein isolate to a food processor and process the ingredients into a smooth mixture.

   Alternatively, add all ingredients to a medium bowl, cover it, and process using a handheld blender.

2. Line a baking sheet with parchment paper to prevent the balls from sticking to the plate.

3. Scoop out a heaping tablespoon of the chocolate hazelnut mixture and roll it into a firm ball using your hands. Repeat the same process for the other 11 balls.

4. Place the cocoa powder in a medium bowl. Roll the balls in the cocoa, then transfer them to the baking sheet.

5. Put the baking sheet in the fridge for about 45 minutes, until all the balls have firmed up.

6. Take the baking dish out of the fridge and store the hazelnut chocolate balls or serve them right away with the optional toppings and enjoy!

7. Store the chocolate balls in an airtight container in the fridge, and consume within 6 days. Alternatively, store the balls in the freezer, using Ziploc bags, for a maximum of 90 days and thaw the at room temperature.

NOTE: No blender? Mince the dates and nuts as fine as possible, knead all the ingredients by hand and add a quarter cup of water to make everything stick together.

8. ALMOND COOKIE BALLS

Serves: 12 balls   ⏱ Cook: 15 min.   ⏱ Total: 1 hr.

INGREDIENTS:

280 g. | 2 cups
Almonds
(raw and unsalted)

8 dates
(pitted)

40 g. | ¼ cup
Raisins

60 g. | 2 scoops
Organic pea protein

50 g. | ½ cup
Shredded coconut

OPTIONAL TOPPINGS:

Coconut whipped cream
(See recipe on page 34)

Cocoa powder

ALLERGENS

Almonds
(can be substituted
with pumpkin seeds)

METHOD:

1. Preheat the oven to 257°F/125°C and line a baking sheet with parchment paper.

2. Put the almonds on the baking sheet and roast them for about 10 to 15 minutes or until they're fragrant.

3. Meanwhile, cover the dates with water in a small bowl and let them sit for about 10 minutes. Drain the dates after soaking and make sure no water is left.

4. Add the almonds, dates, pea protein raisins and shredded coconut to a food processor and blend into a chunky mixture.

   Alternatively, add all ingredients to a medium bowl, cover it, and process using a handheld blender.

5. Scoop out a heaped tablespoon of the almond mixture and roll it into a firm ball using your hands and place them on the baking sheet lined with parchment paper.

6. Repeat the same process for the other 11 balls.

7. Put the baking sheet in the fridge for about 45 minutes, until all the balls have firmed up.

8. Serve the cookie balls with the optional toppings and enjoy!

9. Store the balls in an airtight container in the fridge and consume within 6 days. Alternatively, tore in the freezer for a maximum of 90 days and thaw at room temperature.

NOTE:
No blender? Mince the dates and nuts as fine as possible and whisk all the ingredients by hand.

9. PISTACHIO PROTEIN ICE CREAM

Serves: 8   🕐 **Total:** 1 hr. 20 min.

INGREDIENTS:

400 ml. | 1 can
Low-fat coconut milk

10 medjool dates
(pitted)

60 g. | 2 scoops
Organic pea protein

15 ml. | 1 tbsp.
Vanilla extract

50 g. | ½ cup
Pistachios
(shelled)

OPTIONAL TOPPINGS:

Pomegranate seeds

Fresh mint

Chopped dark chocolate

ALLERGENS

Pistachios
(can be substituted
with sesame seeds)

METHOD:

1. Add all ingredients to a blender and blend into a smooth mixture.

   Alternatively, add all ingredients to a medium bowl, cover it, and process using a handheld blender.

1. Freeze the mixture for 15 minutes, then stir it and freeze for another 10 minutes.

2. Add any desired toppings and freeze for at least 2 hours.

3. Store the ice cream in the freezer for a maximum of 90 days and thaw for 5 minutes at room temperature before serving.

NOTE:
No blender?
Mince the dates as fine
as possible, knead all the
ingredients by hand and
add a quarter cup of water
to make everything stick
together.

10. PEANUT BUTTER CHOCOLATE BARS

Serves: 8 bars   ⏱ **Cook:** 25 min.   ⏱ **Total:** 1 hr. 20 min.

INGREDIENTS:

260 g. | 1 cup
Peanut butter

10 medjool dates
(pitted)

90 g. | 1 cup
Instant oats

60 g. | 2 scoops
Organic pea protein

100 g. | ½ cup
Dark chocolate
(crushed)

120 ml. | ½ cup
Water

OPTIONAL TOPPINGS:

Peanut butter

ALLERGENS

Peanuts
(can be substituted
with almonds or pumpkin seeds)

METHOD:

1. Preheat the oven to 257°F/125°C.

2. Add the oats, 5 medjool dates and half of the water to a food processor and blend into a smooth mixture.

   Alternatively, add the ingredients to a medium bowl, cover it, and process using a handheld blender.

3. Line a loaf pan with parchment paper. Add the oats mixture to the loaf pan, spread it out and press it down firmly until it is 0.3 inch (1 cm) thick all over.

4. Add the pea protein, peanut butter, the remaining dates and water to a food processor and blend into a smooth mixture.

   Alternatively, add the ingredients to a medium bowl, cover it, and process using a handheld blender.

5. Add the peanut butter mixture in an even layer about 1-inch (2,5 cm) thick on top of the oats layer and press it down firmly to make it stick.

6. Transfer the loaf pan to the oven and let it bake for about 15 minutes.

7. Take the loaf pan out of the oven and add an even layer of the crushed dark chocolate on top.

8. Bake for another 10 minutes, take the loaf pan out of the oven, let it cool down and transfer to the fridge to let the mixture completely firm up for about 45 minutes.

9. Divide into 8 bars, serve cold with the optional peanut butter and enjoy!

10. Store the bars in an airtight container in the fridge, and consume within 6 days. Alternatively, store in the freezer for a maximum of 90 days and thaw at room temperature.

TE: *No blender?
Mince the dates and
nuts as fine as possible,
knead all the ingredients
by hand and add a quarter
cup of water to make
everything stick
together.*

11. GINGERBREAD PROTEIN BARS

Serves: *8 bars*   ⏱ **Cook:** *15 min.*   ⏱ **Total:** *1 hr.*

INGREDIENTS:

280 g. | 2 cups
Almonds
(raw and unsalted)

10 dates
(pitted)

40 g. | 4 tbsp.
5-spice powder

60 g. | 2 scoops
Organic soy isolate
(chocolate flavor)

40 g. | 4-inch piece
Ginger
(minced)

OPTIONAL TOPPINGS:

Cocoa powder

Shredded coconut

ALLERGENS

Soy protein
(can be substituted
with pea protein)
Almonds
(can be substituted
with sunflower seeds)

METHOD:

1. Preheat the oven to 257°F/125°C and line a baking sheet with parchment paper.

2. Put the almonds on the baking sheet and roast them for about 10 to 15 minutes or until they're fragrant.

3. Meanwhile, cover the dates with water in a small bowl and let them sit for about 10 minutes. Drain the dates after soaking and make sure no water is left.

4. Add the almonds, dates, 5-spice powder, protein powder and ginger to a food processor and blend into a smooth mixture.

   Alternatively, add all ingredients to a medium bowl, cover it, and process using a handheld blender.

5. Line a loaf pan with parchment paper. Add the almond mixture to the loaf pan, spread it out and press it down firmly until it is 1 inch (2.5 cm) thick all over.

6. Put the loaf pan in the fridge for about 45 minutes, until it has firmed up.

7. Divide into 8 bars, serve cold with optional toppings and enjoy!

8. Store the bars in an airtight container in the fridge, and consume within 6 days. Alternatively, store in the freezer for a maximum of 90 days and thaw at room temperature.

NOTE: No blender? Mince the dates and nuts as fine as possible, knead all the ingredients by hand and add a quarter cup of water to make everything stick together.

12. QUINOA ALMOND COOKIES

INGREDIENTS:

210 g. | 1½ cups
Almonds
(raw and unsalted)

10 dates
(pitted)

45 g. | ¼ cup
Quinoa
(dry)

90 g. | 1 cup
Instant oats

40 g. | ¼ cup
Chia seeds

120 ml. | ½ cup
Water

OPTIONAL TOPPINGS:

Coconut whipped cream
(See recipe on page 34)

Cocoa powder

Shredded coconut

ALLERGENS

Almonds
(can be substituted
with pumpkin seeds)

METHOD:

1. Preheat the oven to 257°F/125°C, line a baking tray with parchment paper and set it aside.

2. Add all ingredients to a food processor and process until smooth, scraping down the sides of the container if necessary.

   Alternatively, add all ingredients to a medium bowl, cover it, and process using a handheld blender.

3. Take a tablespoon of the mixture, put it on the baking tray lined with parchment paper and press it down to form a 0.6 inch (2 cm) thick cookie.

4. Repeat the process for the remaining cookie dough and make sure there is a bit of space between each cookie.

5. Transfer the baking tray to the oven and bake the cookies for about 12 minutes, until the cookies have set.

6. Take the cookies out of the oven and let them cool down before serving.

7. Serve the cookies with the optional toppings and enjoy!

8. Store the cookies in an airtight container in the fridge and consume within 3 days. Alternatively, store in the freezer for a maximum of 30 days and thaw at room temperature.

CONCLUSION

Now that you're equipped with these 76 high-protein recipes, getting enough protein from plant-based foods will be a piece of cake. As a bonus, these storage-friendly five-ingredient dishes mean that you'll free up time you would otherwise have spent cooking, shopping for ingredients, or worrying about your protein intake.

If you're ready for the next step on your journey and want to focus even more on building muscle or losing weight, check in with us for a free consultation!

http://happyhealthygreen.life/free-consultation

Apply here and we'll help you calculate your calorie and macronutrient needs. If you're interested, we can help you with your nutrition game plan and fitness strategy too.

We offer both standard and custom high-protein meal plans that incorporate the five-ingredient recipes from this book alongside other easy-to-prepare dishes. For more information and pricing, check out our free and paid plans on our website here: ***http://happyhealthygreen.life/meal-plans***

You can also find and follow us on social media.

f *https://www.facebook.com/happyhealthygreen.life*

https://www.instagram.com/happyhealthygreen.life

https://www.reddit.com/r/HappyHealthyGreen

Before you go, please consider writing a review for this cookbook on Amazon. We read every one of the reviews and take everything to heart, so we really do appreciate you taking the time to help others make a well-informed decision!

The HappyHealthyGreen team.

FREE 5-INGREDIENT MEAL PLANS

Have you ever considered a plan that *calculates all your daily meals for you?*

Good news!

We have four FREE meal plans that include a grocery list and vegan supplement recommendations!

These plans complement the recipes in this cookbook, guarantee proper nutrition and an easy shopping experience with no more than 5 ingredients per meal.

We have a **standard 2000kcal, standard 2500kcal, soy-free 2000kcal & soy-free 2500kcal** 5-ingredient high-protein meal plan, which you can find here:

https://tinyurl.com/mealplan5HP

Choose one, and we'll drop a printable PDF-file - that calculates all your meals according to your caloric needs - right in your inbox...

Plus, some awesome tips to help you live your best life! (We *hate spam and will never email you more than twice a week.*)

Looking to share your results or questions? The 'Plant-Based Fitness & Vegan Athletes' Facebook group is where you connect with us and other athletes. Get inspired and join our growing fit and healthy plant-based family here:

https://tinyurl.com/PBathletes

See you inside!

The HappyHealthyGreen team.

Disclaimer

The recipes provided in this book are for informational purposes only and are not intended to provide dietary advice. A medical practitioner should be consulted before making any changes in your diet. Additionally, recipe cooking times may require adjustment depending on age and quality of appliances. Readers are strongly urged to take all precautions to ensure ingredients are fully cooked in order to avoid the dangers of foodborne viruses. The recipes and suggestions provided in this book are solely the opinion of the author. The author and publisher do not take any responsibility for any consequences that may result due to following the instructions provided in this book.

CPSIA information can be obtained
at www.ICGtesting.com
Printed in the USA
LVHW071415270120
644907LV00007B/13